COOK SMART
MICROWAVE

COOK SMART

MICROWAVE

90 fast and fresh energy-saving recipes

DEAN EDWARDS

hamlyn

They say the best recipes are cooked up over nine months, so this book is dedicated to Baby Edwards, who is due in late 2023, and my beautiful daughter Indie. My proudest moments in life have come from being a dad. Indie, you changed my life when I had you and I just know you will be an incredible big sister and role model. I'm excited to see what life has in store for the Edwards family.

CONTENTS

INTRODUCTION

If I polled everyone who owns a microwave and asked them if they use it to its full potential, I have a good feeling that 99.9 per cent would say 'no'. I've been in that boat too, using the microwave only for reheating food, or defrosting it when I've been disorganized and forgotten to take something out of the freezer. We've all been there, trust me. But all our everyday bills are going up and, for the first time, this is leading us to consider not only the price of ingredients, but also the cost of cooking them. At the time of writing this book, cooking in a microwave – just like an air fryer or a slow cooker – is an incredibly energy-efficient method of cooking. Luckily for you, I've written books about all these cooking methods, so take your pick! And because I like to cook with energy-efficient devices, I've seen a big difference in my energy bills.

In fact, the microwave is by far the cheapest method of cooking, and usually the quickest too. But there's much more to microwave cookery than just its affordability. I'm here to tell you that microwaves are an incredibly versatile tool in the kitchen. You can cook all manner of dishes, sweet or savoury, with the press of a couple of buttons. And you only need a minimum of kit, the very basics such as microwave-safe bowls and containers, lids or clingfilm, as well as a probe thermometer for checking when the ingredients are cooked to a safe level.

I've tried my utmost to get the timings in the pages that follow absolutely bang on for you. However, no two electrical appliances are the same – even when they are the same wattage – and no two ingredients are the same either. But although you may need to tweak a few of these recipes to suit your microwave and ingredients, you shouldn't be far off. That's where a probe thermometer comes in handy: use it to see whether ingredients such as meat and fish are cooked, not only to a safe temperature, but also to perfection. There's a good reason why every single professional restaurant in the country uses them.

I've thought long and hard about the perfect balance of recipes for this book. There's a really fine line between doing something for convenience and doing something for the sake of it. As I was writing this book, many, many recipes fell by the wayside. Some because they just don't work. For example: plain old rice. I tried and I tried and I *tried* to make rice work in a microwave and, in the end, I got very close. But I had to consider: is this actually easier than cooking it on the hob? The answer was a resounding 'no'. They make microwave rice for a reason! I really hope that I have got the balance right, combining energy-efficient cookery, cost-effective ingredients and making these recipes convenient, to produce some really incredible flavour-packed recipes that I know you are going to love.

MICROWAVE TIPS

Before you start to cook from this book, it's a good idea to read through your microwave's manual, as this will give you guidance on recommended operating procedures and safety precautions. All of the recipes in this book were tested using an 800-watt E-rated microwave. Depending which model of microwave you have, you might need to reduce the cooking times, or add to them a little more. Microwaves range from 700-watts to 1,200-watts, while newer models are also graded A–E, with E being the most powerful. The higher the wattage, the quicker the food will cook.

———

As I wanted to keep the recipes in this book super simple, I've used a bog-standard microwave to develop these recipes. Nothing fancy, no built-in oven; just a bang-your-food-in-and-wait-for-the-ping type of microwave. As I mentioned above, no two microwaves are the same, so to make things easier for you, all of the recipes in this book have been developed cooking only on the full-power setting.

———

Always make sure that your food is piping hot before eating. I always test the internal temperature of meat and fish, to check they are safe to eat, with a probe thermometer. I've given the temperatures that the meat or fish need to reach within the recipe instructions.

———

I know I've written the instruction into most of the recipes here, but make sure to stir your food halfway through cooking, as this will ensure even heating throughout. It's always sensible to keep in mind that pieces of food of a similar size will cook at a similar rate, so if you're chopping ingredients such as vegetables, cut them all to the same size.

———

It probably goes without saying, but please do not put anything metallic in a microwave. Always use microwave-safe cookware, heatproof glass and ceramic bowls.

———

I've found a microwave-safe plate, or clingfilm with a couple of small holes poked in the top, are the most convenient ways to cover food while it's cooking in the microwave. Please be careful when removing lids, plates or clingfilm during or after cooking, due to the very hot steam that's released, which can lead to serious scalds.

———

Always let food stand inside the microwave for one or two minutes after the cooking time has finished. This allows heat to distribute through the dish, ensuring evenly cooked food and eliminating any hotspots.

———

START THE DAY RIGHT

For me, there are rules about cooking at breakfast time. I don't mind prepping ahead of time to make life easier in the mornings, but what I need in a breakfast recipe is for it to be super easy, incredibly quick and – most importantly – very tasty. The recipes in this chapter have been developed to help you make the most of your microwave in the mornings, to give you the best start to your day. I'm buzzing to share with you some classics such as Eggs Benedict, with not only the eggs perfectly poached in the microwave but also a lightning-quick hollandaise sauce. There are also some exciting new flavour combinations, such as my Apple Pie Porridge and Spicy Masala Scrambled Eggs. What a perfect start to the day.

2 MINS

 4 MINS

 VEGETARIAN

You're either a breakfast person or you're not. I won't lie: I fall under the second category. I never really wake up hungry, so it takes something pretty special to get me excited to eat in the mornings. This porridge is definitely worth getting out of bed for. The smoky cinnamon flavour and sweet apple work perfectly with the creamy porridge oats, topped with crunchy granola for texture. A bowl of this and I'm ready to face the day.

APPLE PIE PORRIDGE

SERVES 1
—

1 apple, peeled, cored
   and cut into 1 cm
   (½ inch) cubes
1 teaspoon butter
1 tablespoon honey, plus
   more (optional) to serve
¼ teaspoon ground
   cinnamon
20 g (¾ oz) raisins
40 g (1½ oz) rolled oats
150 ml (¼ pint) whole milk
1 tablespoon granola

1. Place the cubed apple, butter, honey, cinnamon and raisins into a microwave-safe bowl, cover and cook on full power for 2 minutes.

—

2. Stir well, add the oats and milk, then cover again and cook for a further 2 minutes.

—

3. Leave to stand for 1 minute, then sprinkle over the granola and add a final drizzle of honey to taste, if you like.

—

3 MINS

 1½ MINS

 VEGETARIAN

This recipe just goes to show that a cup of tea isn't the only thing you need in a mug at breakfast time. This is such an easy way to enjoy a sweet treat in the morning. I love to use a croissant in this recipe, but you can also use cubed white bread, or even some torn-up brioche rolls if you have any knocking around. I love to serve this with seasonal berries.

CINNAMON FRENCH TOAST IN A MUG

SERVES 1

1 egg, lightly beaten
2 tablespoons milk
1 tablespoon honey
¼ teaspoon ground cinnamon
1 croissant, torn into pieces (total weight about 60 g/2¼ oz)
seasonal berries, to serve
icing sugar, to dust

1. Take a large microwave-safe mug. In it, whisk together the egg, milk, honey and cinnamon until fully combined.

2. Place in the torn croissant (or see recipe introduction), then mix together. Leave to stand for 1 minute, then give it a gentle stir.

3. Cover with clingfilm, then microwave on full power for 90 seconds. Leave to stand for 1 minute, garnish with seasonal berries, then dust with icing sugar and tuck in.

Tip

Raspberries or blueberries would look and taste good scattered on top of this.

8 MINS

 1½ MINS

A classic breakfast combination if there ever was one, but in this case the eggs are cooked in a buttered ramekin. That way, you get the perfect shape to sandwich in a lovely toasted English muffin. Perfect for a lazy Sunday morning, or a hectic morning on the go.

SMOKED SALMON & EGG MUFFIN

SERVES 1
———

2 eggs, lightly beaten
1 tablespoon chopped chives
knob of butter, plus more
    for the muffin
1 English muffin, halved
40 g (1½ oz) smoked
    salmon slices
salt and pepper

1. Whisk the eggs together with the chives in a microwave-safe bowl, then add a good pinch of salt and pepper. Butter the inside of a ramekin about 10 cm (4 inches) in diameter and 5 cm (2 inches) deep, pour in the eggs, cover with clingfilm, then pop a couple of holes in the top. Cook on full power for around 90 seconds, then leave to stand for 1 minute.
———

2. Meanwhile, toast and butter the muffin.
———

3. Lay the salmon on the base of the muffin, add the egg, then crown with the top of the bun.
———

2 MINS

 4½ MINS

 VEGETARIAN

For some reason, I always end up buying croissants in the supermarket, eating one and then forgetting about them, so when I go back to them they're usually a bit stale. A great tip for refreshing croissants – and stale bread too, for that matter – is just to flash them through the microwave for 15–20 seconds before you want to eat them. Good as new!

CHEESY EGGY CROISSANTS

SERVES 2

20 g (¾ oz) unsalted butter
4 eggs
50 g (1¾ oz) Cheddar cheese, grated
2 tablespoons milk
2 tablespoons chopped chives
2 large croissants
salt and pepper

1. Place the butter in a microwave-safe bowl, then cook on full power for 1 minute until melted.

2. Crack in the eggs, then whisk them into the butter along with the cheese, milk and half the chives. Season with salt and pepper. Cook on full power in 30-second bursts, stirring to break up the eggs after each burst. They should take 2–3 minutes of cooking in total.

3. Slice the croissants horizontally, then warm in the microwave for 30 seconds. Gently fill with the fluffy egg, then sprinkle over the remaining chives and serve.

4 MINS

 5 MINS

 VEGETARIAN

I just love this eggy dish, which has its roots in the food of North Africa and the Middle East. The rich and smoky tomato sauce works perfectly with the eggs, which poach within the sauce, absorbing all those incredible flavours. Simply served with some toasted bread, this a dish worth waking up for on those lazy mornings. This recipe was tested cooking one bowl at a time, so you might need to add some more cooking time if cooking both dishes at once.

ALL-IN-A-BOWL SHAKSHUKA

SERVES 2

400 g (14 oz) can of
   chopped tomatoes
1 teaspoon onion granules
½ teaspoon garlic granules
½ green pepper, deseeded
   and chopped
1 teaspoon smoked paprika
½ teaspoon ground cumin
1 teaspoon sugar
2 eggs
40 g (1½ oz) feta cheese,
   crumbled
salt and pepper
hot buttered toast, to serve

1. Mix together the tomatoes, onion and garlic granules, pepper, spices and sugar, then season with salt and pepper. For best results cook 1 portion at a time. Divide the tomato mixture into 2 small microwave-safe bowls, then microwave on full power for 3 minutes.

2. Stir well, then make a well in the sauce, crack in an egg – not forgetting to prick the yolk with a pin or toothpick – then cover, return to the microwave and cook for 2 minutes, microwaving in 20-second bursts until the white of the egg is set. Repeat to cook the other bowl and the remaining egg.

3. Once cooked, leave to stand for 1 minute, then season to taste, crumble over the feta cheese and serve with toast.

Tip

Pricking the egg yolk prevents it from bursting in the microwave during cooking.

8 MINS

 2½ MINS

This breakfast only used to be on the menu for my family on lazy weekend days, when I had a little bit more time on my hands. But that isn't the case any more, as I can whip it up in just minutes using my trusty microwave. Making hollandaise sauce in the microwave makes this meal so simple to cook, so if you've ever been too frightened to have a go at a tricky classic hollandaise, then this is the recipe you've been waiting for.

EGGS BENEDICT

SERVES 2

4 teaspoons white
   wine vinegar
4 eggs
2 English muffins, halved
butter, for the muffins
2 thick slices of ham
bunch of chives, chopped
salt and pepper

For the hollandaise
2 egg yolks
1 teaspoon white
   wine vinegar
¼ teaspoon cayenne pepper,
   plus more to serve
pinch of salt
110 g (4 oz) unsalted butter
lemon juice, to taste

Tip

When poaching eggs, the fresher the egg, the better the result. The vinegar used in the boiling water when poaching eggs will help set the whites.

1. For the hollandaise, whisk together the yolks, vinegar, cayenne and salt in a microwave-safe bowl. Heat the butter in a microwave-safe jug on full power for 45–60 seconds until melted, then slowly drizzle this into the egg yolks, whisking as you go.

2. Place the bowl in the microwave and cook for 10 seconds, whisk again, then microwave in 10-second bursts, whisking in between each, until the sauce has thickened. This will take 50–60 seconds in total. Check the seasoning and add lemon juice to taste.

3. Now for the poached eggs. Pour boiling water into a microwave-safe mug about halfway up, add 1 teaspoon of vinegar, gently crack in an egg, then cook on full power for 30 seconds. Check to see if the egg is cooked, and, if not, keep cooking in 10-second bursts until the whites are set. Mine usually take 40 seconds. I like to microwave-poach 1 egg at a time for precise results.

4. Meanwhile, toast and butter the muffins, then top each half with a slice of ham, then a poached egg and finally gently spoon over some of the hollandaise sauce. Season to taste and finish with a dusting of cayenne pepper and a sprinkle of chives.

5 MINS

 4 MINS

 VEGETARIAN

Chilli for breakfast anyone? I just love the heat that comes from a fresh chilli, but it doesn't only bring fire to this dish, it also adds a beautiful flavour to the creamy eggs. This is such a quick and easy meal to put together in the morning and, to make it even easier, I always keep a pack of mini garlic naans in the freezer, ready to pop straight into the toaster. They just work perfectly to add texture to a stunning breakfast dish.

SPICY MASALA SCRAMBLED EGGS

SERVES 1

___

15 g (½ oz) unsalted butter
3 eggs
1 green chilli, deseeded
    and finely chopped
¼ teaspoon ground turmeric
½ teaspoon garam masala
1 tablespoon milk
1 mini naan
1 tablespoon chopped
    coriander, plus more
    to garnish
salt and pepper
sliced green chilli, to garnish

1. Pop the butter into a microwave-safe bowl, then cook on full power for 1 minute until melted.

___

2. Crack in the eggs, whisk them in, along with the chilli, spices and milk, then season with salt and pepper. Cook on full power in 30-second bursts, stirring to break up the eggs after each burst. This should take 2–3 minutes of cooking in total. Meanwhile, toast the naan then cut it in half.

___

3. Once the eggs are cooked, stir through the coriander, season to taste and serve with the toasted naan, garnished with more chopped coriander and some sliced green chilli.

___

5 MINS

2 MINS

I remember vividly the first time my Nanny Jack cooked bacon in her microwave when I was a young boy. I think that was actually my first memory of this new piece of kitchen equipment: I remember wondering how she had cooked it so quickly and perfectly. Not only does a microwave make bacon beautifully crisp, but it's also a healthier way to cook it. I use kitchen paper to absorb the excess fat and stop the microwave from getting splattered.

IN-A-FLASH BLT

SERVES 1

4 smoked streaky bacon rashers
2 slices of sourdough bread
butter, for the bread
1 tablespoon mayonnaise
3 Baby Gem lettuce leaves
1 medium-sized tomato, sliced
salt and pepper

1. Place a sheet of kitchen paper on a microwave-safe plate, place on the bacon rashers, making sure they don't overlap, then place a second sheet of kitchen paper over the top. Cook on full power for 2 minutes. Meanwhile, toast and butter the bread.

2. Build a sandwich on 1 slice of the toast by layering on the mayonnaise, lettuce, tomato and finally the crispy bacon. Season to taste with salt and pepper, then pop on the final piece of toast and enjoy.

Tip

If you like your bacon extra-crispy, add an extra 30 seconds to the cooking time until it's cooked to your liking.

3 MINS

 3 MINS

I've got a soft spot for this recipe, which I guess comes from wanting to eat spiced food for pretty much every meal! I just love how spices add extra dimensions to the most basic ingredients. This cheat's version of kedgeree takes just a few minutes to cook in the microwave, so even on the busiest morning you can enjoy this delicious dish. It's especially good topped with one of my microwave 'Fried' Eggs (see page 56).

3-MINUTE CHEAT'S KEDGEREE

SERVES 1

---

30 g (1 oz) butter
1 heaped teaspoon tikka
    masala paste
½ teaspoon ground turmeric
1 × 250 g (9 oz) pouch of
    microwave basmati rice
90 g (3¼ oz) hot-smoked
    salmon
4 spring onions, sliced
¼ teaspoon chilli flakes,
    or to taste

To serve
lemon wedges
2 'Fried' Eggs (optional,
    see page 56)

1. Pop the butter into a large microwave-safe bowl, then cook on full power for 1 minute. Stir through the tikka masala paste and turmeric, then sprinkle in the pouch of microwave rice and give it another stir. Cover and cook for a further 2 minutes.

---

2. Flake in the hot-smoked salmon, then gently stir all the ingredients together.

---

3. Scatter over the spring onions and chilli flakes, then squeeze over some lemon juice. I love a microwave 'fried' egg with this dish.

3 MINS

 3 MINS

What a great way to start the day! I'm not always hugely organized, so if I need breakfast on the go this super-quick and easy loaded burrito is a great option. Just roll it in foil and off you pop to go about your business. The eggs literally take next to no time to cook, so this breakfast can be made, rolled and in your belly within minutes.

BREAKFAST BURRITO

SERVES 1

———

2 eggs
30 g (1 oz) chorizo,
    very finely chopped
1 tablespoon milk
1 large flour tortilla
½ ripe avocado, peeled,
    pitted and sliced
handful of baby spinach
hot sauce, to taste
salt and pepper

To garnish (optional)
chilli flakes
lemon wedges

1. Beat together the eggs, chorizo and milk in a microwave-safe bowl, then season with salt and pepper. Cook on full power in 30-second bursts, stirring to break up the eggs after each burst. They should take 2–3 minutes of cooking in total.

———

2. Lay a flour tortilla on a flat surface, then spoon the eggs along its length, leaving space by the edge for rolling.

———

3. Layer the avocado and spinach on top of the line of egg. Add hot sauce to taste, and chilli flakes and a squeeze of lime if liked.

———

4. Fold in the sides and roll the burrito up tightly to serve.

———

TAKE TO WORK

What do you take to work for lunch? I'm seriously hoping that soggy sandwiches and packets of crisps are going to be off the menu for you in future, once you've cast your eyes over the delicious recipes in the pages that follow. I was really excited to think outside the box for this chapter, not only in terms of *what* you take to work, but also *how* you cook at work. My wife Liz works in an office and her only way to prepare food is in the microwave. Sure, you can use it to reheat meals, but some of the recipes in this chapter are prepped to be cooked from fresh in the office microwave, such as my On-the-fly Thai-style Rice Salad, Take-to-work Banoffee Porridge and Pimped-up Instant Ramen Noodles: all cooked in just minutes. If you just want to reheat meals that have already been prepped in your microwave at home, there are also a selection of delicious soups, salads and pastas here to cater for all tastes.

3 MINS

 3 MINS

 VEGETARIAN

Sometimes that last 10 minutes in bed is well worth enjoying. I'm definitely prone to hitting the snooze button, but that does mean that I often leave the house late. By having breakfast prepped and ready to go, all I need to do is take it out of the refrigerator and then, when I'm in work, a quick blast in the microwave is all it needs to cook. Before I know it, I'm tucking into a delicious breakfast and ready to start my day.

TAKE-TO-WORK BANOFFEE PORRIDGE

SERVES 1

———

40 g (1½ oz) rolled oats
1 tablespoon caramelized
    biscuit spread, such
    as Biscoff
1 tablespoon honey
200 ml (7 fl oz) whole milk
1 small banana, sliced
30 g (1 oz) dark chocolate
    chips

1. Pop all the ingredients into a sealable microwave-safe container, finishing with the sliced banana and chocolate chips. Keep in the refrigerator until you are ready to eat.

———

2. At breakfast time, cover the container and cook on full power for 3 minutes. Leave to stand for 1 minute before gently stirring and tucking in.

———

8 MINS

 12 MINS

I love cooking vegetables in the microwave: they retain all their fresh and vibrant colour and also, more importantly, their flavour. The combination in this recipe is not new, but it triggers fantastic food memories for me. Salty blue cheese and bacon along with sweet broccoli is the reason I love it. It's a perfect recipe to cook and portion, ready to take to work for lunches throughout the week.

BROCCOLI, BACON & BLUE CHEESE SOUP

SERVES 2

1 medium potato, peeled and chopped (total weight about 180 g/6 oz)
1 onion, chopped
400 ml (14 fl oz) boiling vegetable stock
1 head of broccoli, cut into florets (total weight about 250 g/9 oz)
100 g (3½ oz) smoked bacon
80 g (2¾ oz) blue cheese, crumbled
salt and pepper

To serve
double cream
crusty bread

1. Pop the potato and onion into a microwave-safe bowl, pour in the stock, then cover and cook for 8 minutes on full power, stirring halfway through.

2. Add the broccoli and bacon, then cook for a further 4 minutes.

3. Transfer to a food processor with half the blue cheese, then blitz until smooth. At this point, season with salt and pepper: you might not need much salt, as the blue cheese and bacon are both salty. Portion into bowls, drizzle over some double cream, then serve with the remaining blue cheese crumbled on top. Enjoy with some crusty bread.

4. If taking to work, portion into suitable microwave-safe containers and keep chilled until ready to cook. To reheat, cook on full power for 3 minutes, stirring halfway through.

8 MINS

 8 MINS

 VEGETARIAN

When I first got into cooking as an adult, we used to love throwing Come Dine With Me-style dinner parties. This minted pea soup was one of my go-to starters, I just love it, and – luckily for me – so did my guests. By cooking the peas in the microwave, you retain their beautiful vibrant green colour and, more importantly, their freshness of flavour. Serve with crusty bread and lashings of butter.

MINTED PEA SOUP

SERVES 2

---

200 g (7 oz) potato,
   peeled and cut into
   1 cm (½ inch) cubes
1 teaspoon garlic paste
1 tablespoon oil
200 g (7 oz) frozen peas
4 spring onions, roughly
   chopped (total weight
   about 60 g/2¼ oz)
400 ml (14 fl oz) boiling
   vegetable stock
1 heaped teaspoon
   mint sauce
2 tablespoons double cream,
   plus more to serve
salt and pepper
buttered crusty bread,
   to serve

1. Place the potato, garlic paste and oil into a microwave-safe bowl, season with salt and pepper, then cover and cook on full power for 4 minutes.

---

2. Add the peas and spring onions, cover again and cook for a further 4 minutes.

---

3. Transfer the vegetables to a food processor, then add the boiling stock, mint sauce and cream. Blitz until silky-smooth, then serve with an extra drizzle of double cream and some buttered crusty bread.

Tip

This soup is incredible served with my Parmesan Crisps (see page 143).

8 MINS

 16 MINS

 VEGETARIAN

You can get some absolutely fantastic shop-bought pesto in local shops and I've never been a person who frowns at using ingredients that will not only save you time, but also money. I like to jazz pesto up a little with lemon juice, just to cut the richness. This dish is just as delicious eaten cold at work as it is piping-hot from the microwave.

LEMONY PESTO PASTA

SERVES 2

180 g (6 oz) dried fusilli pasta
200 g (7 oz) Tenderstem broccoli, cut into bite-sized pieces
2 tablespoons shop-bought pesto
finely grated zest and juice of ½ lemon
½ teaspoon chilli flakes
salt and pepper
finely grated Parmesan cheese, to serve

1. Tip the pasta into a microwave-safe bowl or dish, then pour in boiling water, making sure the pasta is completely covered. Cover and cook on full power for 3 minutes longer than the suggested cooking time on the packet. (For example, if the packet states to cook for 11 minutes, cook in your microwave for 14 minutes.) Drain, reserving some of the cooking liquid, then return the pasta to the bowl.

2. Pop the broccoli into another microwave-safe bowl, cover and cook on full power for 2 minutes, then add it to the bowl with the pasta.

3. Spoon in the pesto, then add the lemon zest and juice, chilli flakes and salt and pepper. Stir well to combine, then add a little of the reserved pasta cooking liquid if you like it a bit saucier. Finish with a grating of Parmesan cheese.

Tip

If you are taking this to work, reheat it in the microwave for 2 minutes.

12 MINS

 3 MINS

 VEGETARIAN

You can buy an incredible array of different-flavoured instant ramen noodles now. Not only are they inexpensive, but they are darned tasty too. They're also the perfect candidate for a filling lunch, which you can bulk out with ingredients you may have in your refrigerator or store cupboard. Just prep your containers and take them to work to pop in the microwave. I love to serve ramen with a soft-boiled egg, but those cannot be cooked in a microwave, so boil them in bulk ready to eat with this meal.

PIMPED-UP INSTANT RAMEN NOODLES

SERVES 2
——

2 × 90 g (3¼ oz) packs of instant ramen noodles (flavour of your choice)
150 g (5½ oz) silken tofu, cut into small cubes
2 handfuls of baby spinach
1 teaspoon garlic and ginger paste
3 spring onions, finely sliced
2 × 300 ml (½ pint) boiling water
2 soft-boiled eggs, halved

To serve
chilli flakes
sriracha sauce

1. For this recipe, you will be dividing the ingredients into 2 separate microwave-safe containers. Place the noodles and the flavour sachet ingredients in the separate containers and divide the tofu, spinach, garlic and ginger paste and finally the spring onions between them. Seal with the lids until ready to cook.

——

2. When lunchtime comes around, pour 300 ml (½ pint) of boiling water into each portion of noodles, then cover and cook in the microwave on full power for 3 minutes, stirring halfway through. Leave to stand for 2 minutes before serving with a soft-boiled egg, and a scattering of chilli flakes and a drizzle of sriracha sauce for a chilli kick.

——

10 MINS

 6 MINS

Couscous is an essential ingredient in my store cupboard. But I never cook it according to the packet instructions, by adding just boiling water: that literally tastes like fresh air. I love to inject super-charged flavours by pimping-up stock with smoky paprika-rich chorizo and herbs. This is a great lunch to take to work, or have as a side with a main meal such as my Minted Lamb & Feta Meatballs (see page 105).

SMOKY CHICKPEA & CHORIZO COUSCOUS

SERVES 4
———

400 g (14 oz) can of
   chickpeas, drained
80 g (2¾ oz) chorizo,
   finely sliced
1 tablespoon olive oil
1 teaspoon smoked paprika
1 tablespoon tomato purée
½ teaspoon garlic paste
150 g (5½ oz) couscous
300 ml (½ pint) boiling
   chicken stock
juice of ½ lemon
handful of flat leaf parsley
   leaves, chopped
salt and pepper

1. Tip the chickpeas, chorizo, oil, paprika, tomato purée and garlic paste into a large microwave-safe bowl. Cover and cook on full power for 3 minutes.

———

2. Add the couscous and stock, then stir until well combined. Cover with clingfilm, then return to the microwave to cook for a further 3 minutes.

———

3. Leave to stand for 3 minutes to allow the couscous to finish steaming, then carefully remove the clingfilm. Season with salt and pepper, then add the lemon juice and parsley to serve.

———

12 MINS

 12 MINS

This is a proper packed lunch, full of Caribbean sunshine. We love to be organized in our house, so we have our glass lunch containers on hand with portions of this spicy bake along with rice and seasonal vegetables. This will keep in the refrigerator for up to four days, and also freezes well. If not eating straight away, reheat in the microwave until piping-hot.

CARIBBEAN-STYLE CHICKEN PEPPER BAKE

SERVES 4

400 g (14 oz) skinless
   boneless chicken thighs,
   cut into bite-sized pieces
400 g (14 oz) can of
   chopped tomatoes
1 teaspoon jerk paste
1 teaspoon onion granules
1 teaspoon dried thyme
1 tablespoon garlic
   and ginger paste
1 heaped tablespoon
   tomato purée
1 tablespoon honey
400 g (14 oz) can of
   kidney beans, drained
1 large green pepper,
   deseeded and chopped
4 spring onions, sliced
rice, to serve

1. Place the chicken in a microwave-safe baking dish measuring about 24 × 18 cm (9½ × 7 inches), ensuring the meat is in an even layer.

2. Mix together the tomatoes, jerk paste, onion granules, thyme, garlic and ginger paste, tomato purée and honey, pour this over the chicken, mix well, then cover and cook on full power for 8 minutes, stirring halfway through.

3. Add the beans and pepper, then stir, cover again and cook for a further 4 minutes.

4. Leave to stand for 2 minutes, then scatter over the spring onions and serve with rice.

10 MINS

 2 MINS

My wife Liz likes me to be inventive with her lunches and she definitely keeps me on my toes. I do love the challenge though, and so far I've had no complaints. This is so simple to put together and even easier to finish off while in the office. You just heat the rice in the microwave, then stir through the other ingredients. A super-easy, super-tasty lunch that beats a limp sandwich any day.

ON-THE-FLY THAI-STYLE RICE SALAD

SERVES 2

½ red onion, finely sliced
100 g (3½ oz) cherry
    tomatoes, halved
70 g (2½ oz) sugar snaps,
    halved lengthways
½ under-ripe mango,
    peeled and chopped
150 g (5½ oz) cooked prawns
50 g (1¾ oz) salted peanuts,
    crushed
2 × 250 g (9 oz) pouches of
    microwave jasmine rice
salt and pepper

For the dressing
1 tablespoon mango chutney
1 tablespoon fish sauce
2 tablespoons olive oil
1 tablespoon sweet
    chilli sauce
juice of ½ lime

1. Whisk together all the dressing ingredients, then portion into 2 containers.

2. Mix together the onion, tomatoes, sugar snaps, mango, prawns and peanuts, then divide into 2 sealable containers.

3. At work – or when you're ready to eat – microwave the rice according to the packet instructions, then tip into a bowl of the salad. Season to taste, pour over a container of the dressing and stir well to combine.

Tip

To get extra juice from a fresh lime, pop it into the microwave for 5 seconds before cutting and squeezing.

20 MINS

 7 MINS

I just love a warm chicken salad, and knocking up spiced chicken thighs in my microwave is the simplest way to make one. Like all great salads, this has a fantastic balance in terms of its flavour profile. Sweet, sour and spiced definitely ticks all the boxes for me as a light meal, especially during the warmer months.

CURRIED CHICKEN & MANGO SALAD

SERVES 2

250 g (9 oz) large skinless boneless chicken thighs (about 2)
1 teaspoon mild curry powder
100 ml (3½ fl oz) boiling chicken stock
2 Baby Gem lettuces, leaves separated
¼ red onion, sliced
½ mango, peeled and sliced
salt and pepper
toasted flaked almonds, to serve

For the dressing
3 tablespoons mayonnaise
1 teaspoon mild curry powder
juice of ½ lemon

1. Place the chicken thighs in a microwave-safe baking dish measuring about 20 × 14 cm (8 × 5½ inches), ensuring that they don't overlap. Sprinkle with the curry powder and a pinch of salt and pepper.

2. Pour in the chicken stock, then cover with clingfilm and cook on full power for around 7 minutes. Make sure the internal temperature of the chicken reaches at least 75°C (167°F): use a probe thermometer to do this.

3. Once the chicken is cooked, leave to stand for 5 minutes, then remove from the liquid and shred the meat into bite-sized pieces (discard the cooking liquid).

4. To make the dressing, mix together the mayo, curry powder and lemon juice in a small bowl.

5. Plate up the lettuce, red onion and mango, scatter over the shredded chicken, then drizzle over the dressing and serve with a scattering of toasted flaked almonds.

15 MINS

 2 MINS

 VEGETARIAN

During the warmer months of the year, it's nice to be able to enjoy lunch on the go. This delicious and healthy shawarma-inspired chickpea salad is perfect for picnics, simply cooked at home in the microwave and enjoyed cold at work or in the office (or hopefully in a spot in the sunshine) the following day. Some dishes just taste better the day after making, and luckily this is one of them: it gives the ingredients time to get to know each other.

SHAWARMA CHICKPEA SALAD

SERVES 2

400 g (14 oz) can of chickpeas, drained and rinsed
1 tablespoon olive oil
1 tablespoon shawarma seasoning
½ teaspoon garlic paste
100 g (3½ oz) cherry tomatoes, roughly chopped
¼ cucumber, chopped
½ small red onion, finely chopped
salt and pepper

To serve
hummus
toasted pitta chips

1. Pop the chickpeas into a microwave-safe bowl, drizzle over the oil, then sprinkle over the shawarma seasoning. Add the garlic and a good pinch of salt and pepper, stir well, then cover and cook on full power for 2 minutes. Leave to cool.

———

2. Mix through the tomatoes, cucumber and red onion, then portion into your take-to-work containers.

———

3. Spoon in a nice dollop of hummus and make sure you take toasted pitta chips with you, to help you scoop up this delicious summer salad.

———

15 MINS

 2 MINS

There are lots of occasions when – even though I've been forward-planning enough to put together a lunch – I just know I'm not going to have time to reheat it and eat it hot. This is where recipes such as this come into play, which have already been cooked at home in the microwave to be eaten cold on the move or at work. If you're taking this to the office, decant the dressing into a suitable container and pour it over the salad just before eating.

TERIYAKI TUNA SALAD

SERVES 2

—

2 small tuna steaks
4 tablespoons teriyaki sauce
1 tablespoon olive oil
juice of ½ lime
1 large avocado, peeled, pitted and chopped
90 g (3¼ oz) bag of baby leaf salad leaves
¼ red onion, sliced
1 teaspoon black sesame seeds

Tip

A small squeeze of lime juice will stop the avocado turning brown, if you aren't eating this salad straight away.

1. Place the tuna steaks in a small microwave-safe baking dish, then pour over the teriyaki sauce, cover and cook on full power for 3 minutes.

—

2. Use a probe thermometer to make sure that the tuna has reached an internal temperature of at least 50°C (122°F). Leave the tuna to stand for 2 minutes before flaking into bite-sized pieces.

—

3. Pour off the teriyaki sauce into a small bowl, then add the olive oil and lime juice. Whisk this together to make a dressing.

—

4. Plate up the avocado, salad leaves and red onion, scatter with the flaked tuna, then drizzle over the dressing and sprinkle with the sesame seeds to serve.

—

LIGHTNING LUNCHES

So many people don't maximize lunch. During a busy week, it is sometimes tough to find the time even just to sit down and enjoy a meal, let alone cook one from scratch. I've eaten many lunches on the move and sometimes that means a disappointing bought sandwich, but, if possible, I love to tuck into something delicious at lunchtime. So this chapter is packed with recipes for meals which are very *very* easy to prepare, quick to cook and even faster to reheat for a tasty lunch whether you're at home, work or on the move. Why not give my daughter Indie's favourite Barbecue Pizza a go? I bet you didn't know you can even cook a pizza base from scratch in the microwave! And I do have to implore you to try my favourite lunch snack: Ramen Noodle Steamed Eggs. Please give them a go, you won't regret it.

15 MINS

 16 MINS

 VEGETARIAN

Lunches for work are pretty important in our house, especially for my wife Liz, who only has limited time to grab a bite to eat during her busy day. Soup is a fantastic option and she loves this fragrant and spicy sweet potato soup, which can be cooked in bulk, then portioned into containers ready to be reheated in the microwave at work in the week.

THAI-STYLE SWEET POTATO & COCONUT SOUP

SERVES 4

600 g (1 lb 5 oz) sweet potato, peeled and cut into 2 cm (¾ inch) cubes
1 heaped teaspoon onion granules
1 teaspoon garlic and ginger paste
1 tablespoon Thai red curry paste
400 g (14 oz) can of full-fat coconut milk
200 ml (7 fl oz) boiling vegetable stock
2 tablespoons soy sauce, or to taste
prawn crackers, to serve (optional)

To garnish
coriander leaves
sliced red chilli
coconut oil

1. Pop the sweet potatoes into a microwave-safe bowl, then cover and cook for 10 minutes on full power.

2. Add the onion granules, garlic and ginger paste, Thai curry paste, coconut milk and stock, then cover again and cook for another 6 minutes.

3. Transfer all the ingredients to a food processor, then blitz until silky smooth. Season with the soy sauce to taste, then portion into bowls.

4. Garnish with coriander leaves and red chilli slices, drizzle with coconut oil and serve with prawn crackers, if liked.

15 MINS

 12 MINS

 VEGETARIAN

A classic: such an inexpensive way to pop a delicious and hearty meal on the table. I don't think rules really apply to this recipe: you can normally bang in anything you have lying around in the vegetable drawer and it comes out great. I love that, by microwaving the ingredients, they do not lose any flavour. I do love a smooth soup, but if you like a bit of texture then just pulse-blend this in the processor before serving.

LEEK & POTATO SOUP

SERVES 4

---

1 large leek, shredded
(total weight about
300 g/10½ oz)
600 g (1 lb 5 oz) potatoes,
peeled and chopped
1 teaspoon garlic granules
1 teaspoon wholegrain
mustard
600 ml (1 pint) boiling
vegetable stock
100 ml (3½ oz) double
cream, plus more to serve
salt and pepper

1. Pop the leeks and potatoes into a microwave-safe bowl, then season with salt and pepper. Cover and cook for 12 minutes on full power, stirring halfway through.

---

2. Transfer the vegetables to a food processor along with the garlic granules, mustard, boiling stock and cream, then blitz until smooth.

---

3. Portion the soup into bowls, then serve with a small drizzle of double cream.

---

3 MINS

 2¼ MINS

Who knew you could cook a pizza base from scratch in a microwave? I remember when I was growing up and microwaves were all the rage, you could buy a really tiny deep-dish pizza in the frozen aisle at the supermarket. I'm not sure if you can still get them, but I won't lie: I did love them. This delicious barbecue sauce-based pizza can be on the table in about five minutes... how incredible is that when you're in need of a lightning lunch?

BARBECUE PIZZA

SERVES 1

For the pizza base
80 g (2¾ oz)
   self-raising flour
3½ tablespoons milk
½ teaspoon baking powder
good pinch of salt

For the toppings
1 tablespoon barbecue sauce
40 g (1½ oz) ready-grated
   mozzarella cheese
¼ teaspoon chilli flakes
¼ teaspoon dried oregano
½ × 22 g (¾ oz) mini salami
   stick, such as Peperami
   Hot, sliced
1 spring onion, sliced

1. Start by making the pizza base: weigh all the ingredients into a bowl, mix together, then knead on a clean surface for 30 seconds until it comes together. Roll out to about 18 cm (7 inches) in diameter. Use a fork to prick holes in the dough, then place on a piece of baking parchment and set on a microwave-safe plate. Cook on full power for 45 seconds.

2. Spread the barbecue sauce on to the pizza base, then evenly scatter over the cheese and sprinkle over the chilli and oregano. Arrange over the sliced salami, then return to the microwave to cook for a further 90 seconds.

3. Once cooked, scatter over the spring onion and serve.

10 MINS

 1 MIN

 VEGETARIAN

I know a lot of people think avocado toast is a bit of a fad, but to be honest it is a dish I love and it's so easy to make. This is a quick and delicious lunch or brunch recipe. Cooking the eggs in the microwave has been an absolute revelation, plus you use only a fraction of the oil needed to fry an egg the conventional way. Use whatever type of bread you have in the house for toast, but for me, I'll have a bit of thickly sliced sourdough.

SMASHED AVOCADO TOAST WITH 'FRIED' EGGS

SERVES 2

---

1 avocado
2 slices of bread
1 tablespoon oil
2 eggs
½ teaspoon chilli flakes
salt and pepper

To garnish
lamb's lettuce
olive oil

Tip
For perfect-looking eggs, you can crack them into a small sieve, so the watery egg white runs off, before using.

1. Peel and pit the avocado, scoop the flesh out into a bowl, then smash with a fork, add salt and pepper and stir. Toast the bread and spread it with the avocado.

---

2. For best results, cook the eggs one at a time. Pour half the oil into a small microwave-safe bowl, then crack in an egg. Use a pin or toothpick to gently pop the yolk, then cover with clingfilm, prick a couple of small holes in the top and cook on full power for 30 seconds. If you like your eggs slightly firmer, you can add 10-second bursts until cooked to your liking.

---

3. Leave the first egg to stand for 1 minute, then repeat with the second egg.

---

4. Place the eggs on the smashed avocado-topped toast, season to taste, and then scatter over the chilli flakes. Garnish with some lamb's lettuce and a drizzle of olive oil.

15 MINS

 3 MINS

Let's address the elephant in the room: there was not a single tandoor oven in sight when cooking this recipe. When I head to my local Indian restaurant, I do love tandoori chicken. The beautiful spicy flavours work perfectly with the moist chicken and the char you get from cooking in a super-hot tandoor oven. My microwave version is also delicious and works brilliantly when wrapped up in a fluffy naan with all the trimmings. If you like a chilli kick, you can add some, finely chopped, over the top as well.

'TANDOORI' CHICKEN NAAN WRAP

SERVES 1

1 skinless chicken breast, cut into 2.5 cm (1 inch) pieces
1 medium-sized naan
1 tablespoon mango chutney
Kachumber Salad
    (see page 134)
Mint Raita (see page 120)
salt and pepper

For the marinade
1 heaped teaspoon
    korma paste
1 teaspoon curry powder
¼ teaspoon chilli powder
½ teaspoon ground turmeric
½ teaspoon salt
1 heaped teaspoon garlic
    and ginger paste

To garnish
coriander leaves
lemon wedges
finely chopped red chilli
    (optional)

1. Pop the chicken into a bowl, then add all the ingredients for the marinade. Stir well to combine, then space out the chicken pieces on a microwave-safe plate, cover and cook on full power 3 minutes.

2. Leave to stand for 1 minute. Make sure, using a probe thermometer, that the chicken has reached an internal temperature of at least 75°C (167°F).

3. Warm the naan, then spread on some mango chutney, top with the chicken pieces, kachumber salad and finally a drizzling of mint raita.

4. Season to taste and serve garnished with coriander leaves, lemon wedges for squeezing over, and finely chopped red chilli, if you like.

10 MINS

 7 MINS

A delicious recipe all cooked in one dish inside the microwave. I've taken inspiration from one of my favourite dishes, with its iconic three ingredients that work together more perfectly than any other combo, in my humble opinion. Tomato, mozzarella and basil with the addition of a juicy meatball are perfect to be sandwiched in a soft sub roll.

CAPRESE MEATBALL SUB

SERVES 4

500 g (1 lb 2 oz) minced beef
1 tablespoon onion granules, plus 1 teaspoon
1 teaspoon chilli flakes
1 teaspoon garlic granules
200 ml (7 fl oz) tomato passata
1 tablespoon balsamic vinegar
1 tablespoon dried oregano
1 heaped teaspoon sugar
1 heaped teaspoon cornflour
100 g (3½ oz) ready-grated mozzarella cheese
4 small sub rolls
salt and pepper
basil leaves, to serve

1. In a bowl, mix together the beef, the 1 tablespoon of onion granules, the chilli flakes and garlic granules along with a pinch of salt and pepper. Form into 12 equal-sized meatballs, then place them into a microwave-safe baking dish measuring about 24 × 18 cm (9½ × 7 inches).

2. In another bowl, mix the tomato passata, the 1 teaspoon of onion granules, the balsamic, oregano and sugar. In a cup, mix the cornflour with 1 tablespoon of water until smooth, then stir it into the tomato mixture and pour it over the meatballs.

3. Cover and cook on full power for 5 minutes.

4. Gently stir, scatter over the cheese, then return to the microwave to cook uncovered for a further 2 minutes. Leave to stand for 1 minute. Use a probe thermometer to ensure that the meatballs have reach an internal temperature of at least 71°C (160°F).

5. Meanwhile, toast the sub rolls.

6. Portion the meatballs in their cheesy tomato sauce into the toasted sub rolls, then tear over some basil leaves to serve.

8 MINS

 4 MINS

I just adore this incredibly fragrant and spicy broth. It's a speedy laksa that literally only takes five minutes from start to finish, so when you need a delicious bowl of loveliness in a hurry, this is the recipe to turn to. I've been obsessed with laksa ever since I saw my mate, the MasterChef champion Ping Coombes, cook this on TV. Laksa paste is a great shortcut for a speedy meal and a fantastic addition to your store cupboard.

5-MINUTE PRAWN LAKSA

SERVES 2

———

2 × 50 g (1¾ oz) nests of
    vermicelli rice noodles
400 g (14 oz) can of
    coconut milk
200 ml (7 fl oz) chicken stock
1 heaped tablespoon
    laksa paste
1 teaspoon garlic and
    ginger paste
1–2 tablespoons soy sauce
150 g (5½ oz) cooked prawns
2 handfuls of beansprouts
juice of ½ lime
sliced red chilli, to garnish

1. Soak the rice noodles in boiling water for 5 minutes, then drain and divide between 2 bowls.

———

2. Pour the coconut milk and stock into a large microwave-safe bowl, stir through the laksa paste, garlic and ginger paste and soy sauce, cover then cook on full power for 3 minutes.

———

3. Stir well, then add the prawns and beansprouts, cover again and cook for 1 further minute.

———

4. Add lime juice to taste, then ladle the broth over the rice noodles. Serve garnished with red chilli slices.

———

Tip

If you can't find laksa paste, replace it with the same quantity of Thai red curry paste.

5 MINS

 3 MINS

 VEGETARIAN

I just love the cups of instant ramen noodles you can now find in the world foods aisle of supermarkets. There are so many different flavours to choose from; the one thing I always insist on is that mine need to be spicy. I first came across this ingenious hack online. It's a great way to use up the highly flavoured liquid that gets left in the cup after you demolish the noodles. I always thought it was a massive shame to throw this away, and now you don't have to. What you get, after you cook the eggs in the noodle liquid in the microwave, is the most delicious, flavourful spicy steamed egg soufflé. Trust me, it sounds crazy, but it is brilliant. This protein-rich snack is perfect for when I get back from the gym.

RAMEN NOODLE STEAMED EGGS

SERVES 1

---

1 × 68 g (2½ oz) cup of
   instant ramen noodles
   (flavour of your choice)
200 ml (7 fl oz) boiling water
2 eggs, lightly beaten
1 tablespoon chopped chives
chilli oil, to serve (optional)

1. Remove the lid from the ramen noodle cup, then pour in the boiling water. Cover and leave to sit for 2 minutes so the noodles can rehydrate. When they're ready, eat the noodles but keep the liquid.

---

2. Use a fork to whisk the egg and chives through the noodle liquid, transfer to a microwave-safe bowl, then cover and cook on full power for 3 minutes.

---

3. Let the eggs cool for 3–4 minutes before drizzling over some chilli oil, if liked, and tucking in.

5 MINS

9 MINS

Egg noodles as a side dish was a staple in our household when I was growing up, and they remain a great and inexpensive way to bulk out a delicious meal. The noodles pick up all the flavour from the garlic and soy marinade, used here to cook the salmon to perfection in the microwave. I love to serve this with a sprinkling of sliced spring onions and black sesame seeds for texture. This is a dish my wife Liz loves to take to work and reheat in the microwave for lunch.

STICKY GARLIC & SOY SALMON

SERVES 2

2 small skinless salmon fillets, each about 130 g (4½ oz)
1 heaped teaspoon garlic and ginger paste
2 tablespoons soy sauce
2 tablespoons sweet chilli sauce, plus extra to serve
1 tablespoon rice vinegar
2 medium egg noodle nests
4 spring onions, shredded
1 teaspoon black sesame seeds
lime slices, to garnish

1. Place the salmon in a small microwave-safe baking dish measuring about 20 × 15 cm (8 × 6 inches). Whisk together the garlic and ginger paste, soy sauce, sweet chilli sauce and vinegar, then pour this over the salmon, cover and cook on full power for 4 minutes. Use a probe thermometer to make sure the salmon has reached an internal temperature of at least 50°C (122°F).

2. Pop the noodle nests into a microwave-safe bowl, cover with boiling water, then cover the bowl with clingfilm. Cook on full power for 5 minutes, stirring halfway through. Drain.

3. Serve the salmon on top of the noodles, then drizzle over the sauce and scatter with the spring onions and sesame seeds. Serve with extra sweet chilli sauce and garnish with lime slices.

10 MINS

 6 MINS

Jambalaya is a rice dish which has its origins in the America's Deep South. The flavours are influenced by French and Spanish cuisines and there are many variations. My cheat's version contains the usual smoky flavours associated with this famous recipe, but can be prepped and cooked in mere minutes.

CHEAT'S JAMBALAYA

SERVES 2

50 g (1¾ oz) chorizo, finely chopped
1 green pepper, deseeded and finely chopped
1 teaspoon garlic paste
1 tablespoon vegetable oil
1 heaped teaspoon Cajun seasoning, plus more to serve
1 tablespoon tomato purée
50 ml (1¾ fl oz) chicken stock
2 × 250 g (9 oz) pouches of microwave rice
150 g (5½ oz) raw prawns
salt and pepper
4 spring onions, finely chopped, to garnish
lemon wedges, to serve

1. Pop the chorizo, pepper, garlic paste and oil into a large microwave-safe bowl, then cover and cook for 3 minutes on full power.

2. Once cooked, add the Cajun seasoning, tomato purée and stock, then stir well. Scatter in the rice and prawns, stir gently, then cover again and cook for a further 3 minutes.

3. Leave to stand for 1 minute, then stir again, add salt and pepper to taste, then portion into bowls. Garnish with a sprinkling of spring onions and serve with extra Cajun seasoning and lemon wedges.

SPEEDY SUPPERS

This chapter is for those moments when you haven't got the energy to cook, but you want to put some fantastic food on the table. I've included a recipe that will probably get me in serious trouble with the purists: my microwave Spaghetti Carbonara. Trust me, it's an absolute revelation. I secretly tested it on my wife Liz and she thought it was not only delicious, but had no idea it had been cooked in the microwave. The Butternut Squash & Blue Cheese Risotto is incredibly tasty and my Creamy Chorizo Rigatoni is a must-try. I hope some of these recipes will become firm family favourites for you, just as they have in my household.

12 MINS

 15 MINS

My Nanny Jack is one of those incredible grandmothers who thought her sole purpose on Earth was to feed everyone. You couldn't pop into her house without basically being fed a full dinner, even if you weren't hungry. One of the things I used to eat often at her house was a hearty bowl of lentil soup. I just love the texture and flavour and it always filled me up. I have to admit the addition of the chorizo in this recipe is mine, for the simple reason that I love it.

NANNY JACK'S LENTIL SOUP

SERVES 2

100 g (3½ oz) split red lentils
30 g (1 oz) butter
1 onion, chopped
250 g (9 oz) carrots
450 ml (16 fl oz) boiling
    vegetable stock
30 g (1 oz) chorizo sausage,
    finely chopped
1 tablespoon vegetable oil
salt and pepper
crusty bread, to serve

1. Wash the lentils in plenty of cold water until the water runs clear. Pop into a large microwave-safe bowl, then add the butter, onion, carrots and stock. Stir, then cover and cook on full power for 14 minutes, stirring halfway through.

___

2. Transfer to a blender, then blitz until smooth-ish, though I like a bit of texture left in my soup. Season well with salt and pepper.

___

3. Meanwhile, pop the chorizo and oil into a small microwave-safe bowl, then cook on full power for 1 minute.

___

4. Portion the soup into bowls, then top with some of the chorizo and a drizzle of the chorizo oil from the bowl. Serve with some crusty bread.

___

12 MINS

 18 MINS

Italian food relies on great ingredients and simple combinations to create the most beautiful-tasting dishes. I just love that there is no messing and no compromise when it comes to their cuisine. That's why I'm probably going to have to make an apology for this completely unauthentic amatriciana sauce, but it tastes so good tossed through your favourite pasta. I really enjoy the sauce with very thin spaghetti and a decent grating of Parmesan cheese.

SPAGHETTI AMATRICIANA

SERVES 4

150 g (5½ oz) smoked bacon lardons
1 tablespoon olive oil
1 onion, finely chopped
1 heaped teaspoon garlic paste
400 g (14 oz) can of chopped tomatoes
1 tablespoon tomato purée
1 teaspoon chilli flakes
1 heaped teaspoon dried rosemary
2 tablespoons Worcestershire sauce
1 heaped teaspoon sugar, or to taste
salt and pepper

To serve
360 g (12 oz) cooked spaghetti
finely grated Parmesan cheese
basil leaves

1. Place the bacon in a microwave-safe bowl, then place a sheet of kitchen paper over the top and cook on full power for 3 minutes.

2. Remove the bacon from the bowl, then add the oil, onion, garlic paste, tomatoes, tomato purée, chilli flakes, rosemary and Worcestershire sauce, add a pinch of salt and pepper, then stir well, cover and cook for 10 minutes.

3. Crush the tomatoes with a fork or a potato masher until you have a nice saucy consistency, then return the bacon, cover again and cook for a further 5 minutes.

4. Add the sugar to taste, then toss the sauce through the spaghetti. Serve with grated Parmesan cheese and a sprinkling of basil leaves.

Tip

Add a little of the pasta cooking water to the sauce. This starchy liquid will not only flavour the sauce, but also thicken it.

15 MINS

 17 MINS

 VEGETARIAN

A great combination of sweet butternut squash and sharp blue cheese comes to life in this super-simple microwave risotto. I just cannot begin to tell you how easy it is to make in your microwave, so if you are a fan of a classic Italian risotto, but don't normally cook it – due to having to stand at the stove, constantly stirring the rice – then this recipe is for you. I've also got a great recipe later in this book for a Pea & Leek Risotto (see page 155), if you want another version.

BUTTERNUT SQUASH & BLUE CHEESE RISOTTO

SERVES 2

———

200 g (7 oz) butternut
    squash, cut into 1 cm
    (½ inch) cubes
30 g (1 oz) unsalted
    butter, plus 30 g (1 oz)
1 teaspoon garlic paste
150 g (5½ oz) arborio rice
500 ml (18 fl oz) boiling
    vegetable stock
50 g (1¾ oz) blue
    cheese, crumbled
salt and pepper

1. Pop the butternut squash, 30 g (1 oz) of the butter and the garlic paste into a large microwave-safe bowl, then cook on full power in the microwave for 3 minutes.

———

2. Stir in the rice, making sure it has a good coating of the butter. Pour in half the stock, then stir well, cover and cook on full power for 7 minutes.

———

3. Add the remaining stock, then stir, cover again and cook for a further 7 minutes.

———

4. Once cooked, leave to stand for 2 minutes, then fold through half the blue cheese and the remaining 30 g (1 oz) of butter. Season to taste.

———

5. Portion the risotto into bowls, then crumble over the remaining blue cheese and serve.

———

15 MINS

 6 MINS

Chorizo sausage is a wonderful ingredient that adds its smoky flavour to many dishes. Okay, it's Spanish, while rigatoni is Italian, but I just love it when it releases its delicious oils into this creamy sauce, making it perfect for hugging the pasta. If you like, you can cook the Pasta in the Microwave, too (see page 142).

CREAMY CHORIZO RIGATONI

SERVES 2

180 g (6 oz) dried
   rigatoni pasta
2 cooking chorizo sausages,
   total weight about 180 g
   (6 oz)
1 heaped teaspoon
   garlic paste
1 heaped teaspoon
   dried oregano
1 tablespoon tomato purée
1 tablespoon olive oil
125 g (4½ oz)
   mascarpone cheese
salt and pepper

To serve
chilli flakes, to taste
basil leaves

1. Cook the pasta according to the packet instructions (or see recipe introduction).

2. Skin the sausages, then place them into a microwave-safe baking dish measuring about 24 × 18 cm (9½ × 7 inches). Break the chorizo meat up into small pieces, then add the garlic paste, oregano and tomato purée. Stir well, then season with salt and pepper.

3. Drizzle with the oil, then cover with a sheet of kitchen paper and cook on full power for 4 minutes. Once cooked, stir through the mascarpone and pop it back in the microwave for 2 minutes.

4. Drain the pasta, but reserve some of the cooking liquid. Stir the pasta through the sauce, then add enough of the reserved liquid until you have a silky-smooth sauce coating the pasta.

5. Portion into bowls, then serve with some chilli flakes and basil leaves.

18 MINS

 3 MINS

I'm betting that you've seen many versions of this classic Italian recipe over the years. I've witnessed the internet go into meltdown in reaction to some of them, too. I'm also betting that you have never seen a spaghetti carbonara cooked in the microwave before. I can honestly say that this is just as good as the authentic dish, with the added bonus of hardly any effort.

SPAGHETTI CARBONARA

SERVES 2

---

180 g (6 oz) spaghetti
2 garlic cloves, peeled
100 g (3½ oz) smoked
   bacon lardons
1 tablespoon olive oil
70 g (2½ oz) Parmesan
   cheese, finely grated,
   plus more to serve
2 egg yolks
salt and pepper

1. Cook the pasta according to the packet instructions, or use my Pasta in the Microwave recipe (see page 142). Drain, but reserve some of the cooking liquid.

---

2. Gently crush the garlic cloves down with the flat of a knife, but keep them whole, then place the bacon, garlic and oil in a microwave-safe bowl, cover with a sheet of kitchen paper and microwave on full power for 3 minutes.

---

3. Remove the kitchen paper and the garlic cloves, then add the drained pasta and stir.

---

4. Separately stir together the Parmesan and egg yolks, then add 6 tablespoons of the pasta cooking liquid and stir to make a paste. Add this to the pasta, then stir well, adding more of the starchy pasta water until the spaghetti has a lovely covering of the cheesy sauce.

---

5. Season with salt and pepper, then serve in bowls with some more Parmesan.

10 MINS

 14 MINS

 VEGETARIAN

Who doesn't love a good old mac and cheese? This is actually my daughter Indie's favourite meal, so it's often on the menu for us. I admit that a nice crispy-chewy crust on mac and cheese is great, but you can't get that in the microwave, I'm afraid, so this recipe is for those occasions when I really haven't got the time on my hands. I just love how easy this meal is to put together and it cooks in the microwave all in one bowl, which saves on washing up. Minimum fuss, maximum cheesy flavour.

MICROWAVE MAC & CHEESE

SERVES 2
———

160 g (5¾ oz) dried
    macaroni pasta
1 heaped teaspoon cornflour
170 ml (6 fl oz) milk
50 g (1¾ oz) Cheddar
    cheese, grated
50 g (1¾ oz) ready-grated
    mozzarella cheese
1 teaspoon wholegrain
    mustard
2 tablespoons chopped
    chives

1. Tip the pasta into a large microwave-safe bowl, then pour in enough boiling water to ensure it is completely covered. Cover and cook on full power for 10 minutes, stirring halfway through. Drain the pasta, then return it to the bowl.

———

2. In a cup, mix the cornflour with 1 tablespoon of the milk to a smooth paste. Add this to the pasta with the remaining milk, both cheeses and the mustard. Stir well.

———

3. Cover again and cook for a further 4 minutes. Leave to stand for 2 minutes, then stir well and portion into bowls.

———

4. Finally, scatter with a good amount of chives and serve.

———

5 MINS

 3 MINS

I tried as best I could to keep the cooking method of every recipe in this book microwave-only. That can still be the case if you cook up some of those 'microchip'-style microwave fries for this recipe, but – let's be honest – though they are good in a bind, they don't really compare to fries cooked in the air fryer, oven or (dare say it) deep-fryer. This recipe for pepperoni pizza melt loaded on to fries was just too good not to include. You will forgive me when you taste them.

PEPPERONI PIZZA LOADED FRIES

SERVES 2

100 g (3½ oz) Cheddar cheese, grated
100 g (3½ oz) ready-grated mozzarella cheese
1 teaspoon dried oregano
½ teaspoon chilli flakes
1 × 22 g (¾ oz) mini salami stick, sliced (I used Peperami Hot)
crispy fries

1. Scatter both cheeses into a microwave-safe shallow baking dish, then sprinkle over the oregano, chilli flakes and finally the salami.

2. Cover and cook on full power for 3 minutes until melted.

3. Carefully pour the melt over some hot and crispy fries.

15 MINS

 6 MINS

Britain's favourite curry, recreated in your own home in minutes in the microwave. Tikka masala was a recipe actually invented in the UK. Mild in spice but packed full of flavour, you can see why this creamy and delicious curry works so well with a portion of fluffy basmati rice and some crispy poppadums on the side. I make this version as is and then, once I dish up, I add some fresh chilli to mine just to take the heat levels up. You know I like it hot.

CHICKEN TIKKA MASALA

SERVES 2

2 skinless chicken breasts,
   cut into 2.5 cm (1 inch)
   pieces
200 ml (7 fl oz) tomato
   passata
50 ml (1¾ fl oz) double
   cream, plus more to serve

For the marinade
1 tablespoon butter or ghee,
   melted in the microwave
1 heaped tablespoon
   tikka masala paste
1 heaped teaspoon
   curry powder
1 teaspoon paprika
½ teaspoon ground turmeric
1 heaped teaspoon garlic
   and ginger paste

To serve
steamed rice
finely chopped coriander
finely chopped red chilli
mango chutney
crispy poppadums

1. Mix together all the marinade ingredients in a microwave-safe dish and fold in the chicken pieces. Space out the chicken into a single layer, then cover and cook on full power for 2 minutes. Use a probe thermometer to make sure the chicken has reached an internal temperature of at least 75°C (167°F).

2. Pour in the tomato passata and double cream, then stir to combine. Cover again and cook for a further 4 minutes. Once cooked, leave to stand for 1 minute.

3. Serve with rice, a drizzle of double cream, a scattering of chopped coriander, chopped red chilli, mango chutney and crispy poppadums.

15 MINS

 8 MINS

I've always been fascinated by the flavours of Southeast Asia; they're such a beautiful balance of hot, sweet, salty and sour. In my opinion, no dish encompasses this more than pork or chicken satay. The beauty of this recipe is that you can just bung it all in the microwave, let it do its thing... and when you hear that ping, its ready to go. No stress, hardly any work, and the end result is a delicious meal.

PORK & PEANUT SATAY NOODLES

SERVES 2

---

100 ml (3½ fl oz) full-fat coconut milk
1 heaped tablespoon Thai red curry paste
1 tablespoon peanut butter
1 tablespoon fish sauce
1 heaped teaspoon garlic and ginger paste
200 g (7 oz) minced pork
200 g (7 oz) Tenderstem broccoli, cut into bite-sized pieces
150 g (5½ oz) dried flat rice noodles (pad Thai noodles)
2 green bird eye chillies, finely chopped
lime wedges, to serve

1. Pour the coconut milk into a microwave-safe baking dish measuring about 24 × 18 cm (9½ × 7 inches). Add the curry paste, peanut butter, fish sauce and garlic and ginger paste, mix well, then add the minced pork and stir well to combine.

---

2. Cover and cook on full power for 5 minutes. Place the broccoli on top, then cover again and cook for a further 3 minutes. Leave to stand for 2 minutes, then stir well to combine all the ingredients.

---

3. Meanwhile, rehydrate the rice noodles according to the packet instructions (usually soaking them in boiling water for 5 minutes).

---

4. Drain the noodles, then fold them through the sauce and portion into serving bowls. Scatter with the chopped chillies and serve with a couple of lime wedges.

 20 MINS

8 MINS

Steaming fish inside a baking parchment parcel is such an ingenious way of cooking. Classically, the method is called en papillote: all the flavours stay within the parcel, ensuring nothing escapes, while the fish and other ingredients cook beautifully within. Salmon can take bold flavours, so this beautiful harissa and honey dressing both creates steam and glazes the salmon as it cooks. Just bring these parcels to the table, tear them open and tuck in. As a bonus, it even saves on the washing up.

HARISSA SALMON PARCELS

SERVES 2

100 g (3½ oz) couscous
200 ml (7 fl oz) boiling
    vegetable stock
juice of ¼ lemon, plus more
    lemon wedges to serve
1 tablespoon extra virgin
    olive oil
2 small skinless salmon fillets,
    each about 130 g (4½ oz)
salt and pepper

For the dressing
1 heaped teaspoon rose
    harissa, plus more to serve
1 tablespoon olive oil
juice of ¼ lemon
1 teaspoon honey
80 g (2¾ oz) cherry
    tomatoes, chopped
1 teaspoon dried oregano

1. Place the couscous in a bowl, pour over the boiling stock, cover with clingfilm and leave to stand for 5 minutes. Fork through to separate the grains, season with salt and pepper, then set aside.

2. Mix together the dressing ingredients in a small bowl, then season with salt and pepper.

3. Lay a sheet of baking parchment about 50 cm (20 inches) long on a work surface, then spoon half the couscous over one side. Place on a salmon fillet and drizzle with half the dressing. Fold the parchment over and crimp the edges, pressing tightly to form a seal. Repeat to form the second parcel.

4. Place a parcel on a microwave-safe plate, then cook on full power for 4 minutes. Once cooked, leave to stand for 1 minute. Repeat to cook the second fillet. Use a probe thermometer to make sure the salmon has reached an internal temperature of at least 50°C (122°F).

5. Serve the fish and couscous in the parcels at the table, leaving each person to open their own. Serve with extra lemon wedges and rose harissa.

FAMILY DINNERS

If you've been following me for a while, you know that family-style meals are a huge passion of mine. I truly believe that my love of food comes from growing up in a family where we made the time to sit down and enjoy a meal together. I'm not going to pretend all our meals were like this – because they weren't – but I do really appreciate the times that we did manage it. I guess many people don't know that you can actually cook for a whole family in a microwave. My mission for this chapter was to create hearty and tasty recipes that the family will love. So why not give my Cajun-style Prawn Linguine a try, or one of our most-loved family favourites, Butter Chicken Curry?

20 MINS

 11 MINS

 VEGETARIAN

This Mexican-inspired recipe is made predominantly from cans and store cupboard ingredients. It's always great, when thinking about what to cook for the evening meal, to just use what you have in, rather than having to pop to the shops. The beans add great texture and flavour and, trust me, if you have got into the habit of eating meat every day, try this veggie dish: you will not miss it at all.

SMOKY BEAN ENCHILADAS

SERVES 4

400 g (14 oz) can of kidney beans, drained
400 g (14 oz) can of black beans, drained
1 green pepper, deseeded and chopped
25 g (1 oz) pack of taco seasoning (I use Old El Paso)
500 ml (18 fl oz) tomato passata
4 large flour tortillas
70 g (2½ oz) Mexican cheese, grated
salt and pepper

To serve
crisp salad
soured cream
sliced fresh jalapeño chillies

1. Mix both types of beans, the pepper, taco seasoning and 150 ml (5 fl oz) of the tomato passata in a large microwave-safe bowl, then season with salt and pepper. Stir well until fully combined, then cover and cook on full power for 4 minutes. Leave to stand for 2 minutes.

2. Pour enough tomato passata into a microwave-safe baking dish measuring about 24 × 18 cm (9½ × 7 inches) to cover the bottom; this will stop the enchiladas sticking to the dish.

3. Spoon one-quarter of the bean mixture on to the centre of a tortilla, roll it up, then place in the baking dish. Repeat until the filling is used up and you have 4 stuffed enchiladas, spacing them out in the dish with a gap between each. Pour the remaining passata across the length of the enchiladas, then scatter over the grated cheese.

4. Cook uncovered on full power for 7 minutes. Leave to stand for 2 minutes before serving with a crisp salad, a dollop of soured cream and sliced jalapeño chillies.

15 MINS

 9½ MINS

This tasty curry is a real family pleaser. I do bang on about the benefits of using so-called cheat's ingredients, such as shop-bought curry paste and my favourite garlic and ginger pastes. I know, for many purists, they are not acceptable, but for me they add fantastic amounts of flavour without any effort at all. So, in my book, they're spot on. And did you know that you can cook poppadums in the microwave? Check out my recipe on page 134.

BUTTER CHICKEN CURRY

SERVES 4

50 g (1¾ oz) unsalted butter
400 g (14 oz) skinless boneless chicken thighs, cut into bite-sized pieces
1 tablespoon garam masala
1 teaspoon ground turmeric
1 heaped teaspoon onion granules
1 tablespoon garlic and ginger paste
2 tablespoons korma paste
2 tablespoons tomato purée
100 ml (3½ fl oz) boiling chicken stock
2 teaspoons cornflour
50 ml (3½ fl oz) double cream
salt and pepper

To serve
steamed rice
naan
toasted flaked almonds
coriander leaves

1. Pop the butter into a microwave-safe baking dish measuring about 24 × 18 cm (9½ × 7 inches), then cook on full power for 90 seconds until melted.

2. Add the chicken, spices, onion granules, garlic and ginger paste, korma paste, tomato purée and stock. In a cup, mix the cornflour with 1 tablespoon of cold water to a smooth paste, then stir it in, seasoning with salt and pepper.

3. Ensure the chicken is in an even layer, then cover and cook on full power for 8 minutes, stirring halfway through. Leave to stand for 2 minutes, then stir through the cream. Use a probe thermometer to make sure the internal temperature of the chicken has reached at least 75°C (167°F).

4. Portion into bowls and serve with some rice and naan (or see tip, below), scattered with flaked almonds for texture and coriander leaves for flavour.

Tip

For a lighter option, try this with my low-carb Steamed Cauliflower Rice (see page 136).

18 MINS

 9 MINS

I just love buffalo chicken. It's something I first discovered during a holiday over in the States, but now we're seeing it pop up in cool burger restaurants all over the UK. A good buffalo chicken is only as good as its sauce; in essence, it's hot sauce with butter and garlic... what could be better with chicken? One word of warning: some shop-bought buffalo sauces are very vinegary, so you might need to add a touch more honey to balance the flavour. Simply serve in a toasted bun, with some creamy coleslaw. Banging.

PULLED BUFFALO CHICKEN BAPS

SERVES 4

4 large skinless boneless
   chicken thighs, about
   500 g (1 lb 2 oz)
tablespoons barbecue
   seasoning
about 200 ml (7 fl oz)
   chicken stock
4 tablespoons buffalo sauce
   (see recipe introduction)
30 g (1 oz) butter
1 teaspoon garlic paste
1 tablespoon honey
4 brioche buns
salt and pepper
coleslaw, to serve

Tip

Use an electric
hand whisk on a
low speed to shred
the chicken: it
takes seconds.

1. Season the chicken with the barbecue seasoning, then place into a microwave-safe baking dish measuring about 24 × 18 cm (9½ × 7 inches), ensuring the chicken is in an even layer. Pour in the chicken stock until it comes around one-third of the way up the chicken.

2. Cover and cook on full power for 8 minutes. Make sure the internal temperature of the chicken has reached at least 75°C (167°F), using a probe thermometer. Once cooked, leave to stand for 5 minutes, then remove from the liquid and shred the meat.

3. Tip the buffalo sauce, butter, garlic paste and honey into a small, microwave-safe bowl, heat on full power for 1 minute, then stir well.

4. Meanwhile, toast the brioche buns.

5. Pour the buffalo sauce over the shredded chicken, then stir well to combine and season with salt and pepper. Portion the chicken into the toasted brioche buns and top with creamy coleslaw.

15 MINS

7 MINS

I've fallen in love with this tasty one-dish dinner. Just let the microwave do its work, then finish with some fragrant herbs and almonds for a bit of texture.

CHICKEN SHAWARMA COUSCOUS

SERVES 4

400 g (14 oz) skinless boneless chicken thighs
2 tablespoons shawarma seasoning
100 ml (3½ fl oz) boiling chicken stock, plus 150 ml (¼ pint)
200 g (7 oz) couscous
50 g (1¾ oz) dried apricots
1 tablespoon olive oil
juice of ½ lemon

To serve
50 g (1¾ oz) flaked almonds
chopped coriander
lemon wedges
natural yogurt sprinkled with shawarma seasoning (optional)

1. Cut the chicken into bite-sized pieces, then coat with the shawarma seasoning. Place into a microwave-safe baking dish measuring about 24 × 18 cm (9½ × 7 inches), ensuring the chicken is in an even layer.

2. Pour in the first amount of chicken stock (100 ml/3½ fl oz) until it comes about one-third of the way up the chicken. Cover and cook on full power for 5 minutes. Make sure the internal temperature of the chicken has reached at least 75°C (167°F) with a probe thermometer.

3. Sprinkle in the couscous, stir well, then pour over the second amount of stock (150 ml/¼ pint). Scatter over the apricots, cover again and cook for a further 2 minutes. Leave to stand for 3 minutes to allow the couscous to finish steaming.

4. Add the oil and a squeeze of lemon juice to taste, then scatter over the flaked almonds and chopped coriander and serve with lemon wedges and seasoned natural yogurt, if liked.

15 MINS

 16 MINS

When you're in a bind, pre-cooked chicken – whether it be hot rotisserie from the supermarket counter or pre-cooked and chilled – can be a brilliant time-saver. I just love the flavour that you get from chicken thighs and I use them in all my curries. This fragrant Thai green curry is heavily flavoured with coriander and lemon grass, but there's no need to buy all the individual ingredients, because shop-bought curry pastes are absolutely fantastic to use and they keep for ages in the refrigerator.

GREEN THAI CHICKEN CURRY

SERVES 4

1 onion, chopped
1 heaped teaspoon garlic
  and ginger paste
1 teaspoon vegetable oil
2 tablespoons Thai green
  curry paste
400 ml (14 fl oz) can of
  full-fat coconut milk
2 tablespoons fish sauce
2 tablespoons sugar
1 heaped teaspoon cornflour
150 g (5½ oz) sugar snaps
100 g (3½ oz) frozen peas,
  defrosted
450 g (1 lb) pack of cooked
  chicken thighs, shredded
  and bone removed (total
  weight after preparation
  about 300 g/10½ oz)
juice of 1 lime, plus more
  wedges to serve
steamed jasmine rice,
  to serve
coriander leaves, to garnish

1. Pop the onion, garlic and ginger paste and the oil into a microwave-safe bowl, cover and cook on full power for 4 minutes.

2. Once cooked, stir through the curry paste, coconut milk, fish sauce and sugar, then cover again and cook for a further 4 minutes.

3. In a cup, mix the cornflour with 1 tablespoon of water to a smooth paste, then pour this into the curry, stir well, then throw in the sugar snaps, defrosted peas and shredded chicken.

4. Cover again, then pop back in the microwave to cook for a further 6–8 minutes, or until piping hot. Leave to stand for 1 minute.

5. To finish, add a squeeze of lime juice to taste, then serve scattered with coriander and accompanied by steamed jasmine rice and extra lime wedges.

15 MINS

 8 MINS

These were an absolute favourite of mine growing up. I still remember getting covered in food, as – trust me – there is no tidy way to eat these, but they are well worth the mess. I like to serve mine as my mum did, with shredded lettuce, then the chilli beef, then some tomato and soured cream. So good.

CHILLI BEEF TACOS

SERVES 4
————

400 g (14 oz) minced beef
1 teaspoon garlic paste
1 heaped tablespoon
   tomato purée
25 g (1 oz) pack of taco
   seasoning (I use Old
   El Paso)
1 tablespoon dried oregano
400 g (14 oz) can of kidney
   beans, drained
1 green pepper, deseeded
   and chopped
100 ml (3½ fl oz) beef stock
1 green chilli, deseeded
   and finely chopped
12 crispy taco shells

To serve
shredded lettuce
chopped tomato
lime wedges
soured cream sprinkled with
   taco seasoning (optional)

1. Place the minced beef into a microwave-safe baking dish measuring about 24 × 18 cm (9½ × 7 inches), then use a fork to spread it out into an even layer. Cover and cook on full power for 3 minutes.

————

2. Once cooked, break the beef up again with a fork, then stir through the garlic paste, tomato purée, taco seasoning, oregano, beans, pepper and stock until well combined. Cover again and cook for 5 minutes. Leave to stand for 2 minutes, then add the chilli and mix well.

————

3. Serve in the taco shells, along with some lettuce, tomato, lime wedges and seasoned soured cream, if liked.

————

Tip
This chilli beef would also work great with my Loaded Potato Skins (see page 140).

15 MINS

 7 MINS

There's a big blue furniture store that I quite often visit with the family. When I say 'visit', I mean I'm dragged there, as it's not my idea of a good time at the weekend. But I do look forward to a quick visit to the café, for a good helping of Swedish meatballs and lingonberry jam. Why not give my super-simple microwave version a try and serve it up with my Champ Mashed Potatoes (see page 138)?

SWEDISH-STYLE MEATBALLS

SERVES 4

250 g (9 oz) minced pork
250 g (9 oz) minced beef
2 teaspoons onion granules
100 ml (3½ fl oz) boiling
   beef stock, made from
   a stock pot
1 teaspoon Dijon mustard
1 teaspoon dried dill, plus
   more to serve
1 teaspoon garlic granules
1 heaped tablespoon
   cornflour
50 ml (1¾ fl oz) double cream
salt and pepper

1. Mix together both types of minced meat and half the onion granules along with a pinch of salt and pepper. Form into 16 equal-sized meatballs, then place them into a microwave-safe baking dish measuring about 24 × 18 cm (9½ × 7 inches).

2. In a bowl, stir together the beef stock, Dijon mustard, dill, the remaining onion granules and the garlic granules, add a pinch of salt and pepper then stir well. Pour this into the baking dish. Cover, then cook on full power for 5 minutes.

3. In a cup, mix the cornflour with 1 tablespoon of cold water to a smooth paste, then pour this into the dish with the double cream. Stir well and cook uncovered for a further 2 minutes. Use a probe thermometer to ensure the meatballs have reached an internal temperature of at least 71°C (160°F).

4. Leave to stand for 1 minute, then sprinkle over a little more dill and serve.

15 MINS

 7 MINS

Another one-dish wonder for the family to enjoy. Lamb can be expensive, so using minced lamb here makes it much easier on the wallet. There's something very homely about meatballs, especially when they are spiked with herbs and spices. This Greek-inspired dish is delicious served with my Smoky Chickpea & Chorizo Couscous (see page 40).

MINTED LAMB & FETA MEATBALLS

SERVES 4

—

500 g (1 lb 2 oz) minced lamb
1 heaped teaspoon dried
    oregano
1 teaspoon garlic granules
300 ml (½ pint)
    tomato passata
1 teaspoon onion granules
1 tablespoon dried oregano
1 teaspoon ground cinnamon
1 teaspoon chilli flakes
1 heaped teaspoon sugar
1 tablespoon cornflour
100 g (3½ oz) feta
    cheese, crumbled
salt and pepper

1. Mix together the minced lamb, oregano and garlic granules along with a pinch of salt and pepper. Form into 12 equal-sized meatballs, then place them into a microwave-safe baking dish measuring about 24 × 18 cm (9½ × 7 inches).

—

2. In a bowl, mix the tomato passata, onion granules, oregano, cinnamon, chilli flakes and sugar. In a cup, mix the cornflour with 1 tablespoon of water to a smooth paste, add to the bowl, mix well, then pour the sauce over the meatballs. Cover and cook on full power for 5 minutes, gently stir, then return uncovered to the microwave to cook for a further 2 minutes. Use a probe thermometer to ensure the meatballs have reached an internal temperature of at least 71°C (160°F).

—

3. Leave to stand for 1 minute, before crumbling over the feta to serve.

—

12 MINS

 15 MINS

When I need to throw something together very quickly for dinner, I often reach for the store cupboard. I always seem to have loads of cans in the house and for this recipe you need black beans, tomatoes and sweetcorn. I think they're delicious in a chilli and it's amazing how sometimes the throw-it-all-in dishes seem to work best. I love to serve this with rice, a dollop of soured cream and even a grating of cheese.

SWEET POTATO & CHORIZO CHILLI

SERVES 4

---

300 g (10½ oz) sweet potato, peeled and cut into 1 cm (½ inch) cubes
100 g (3½ oz) chorizo, chopped
400 g (14 oz) can of black beans, drained
400 g (14 oz) can of chopped tomatoes
1 heaped teaspoon smoked paprika, plus more to garnish
1 heaped teaspoon ground cumin
1 teaspoon chilli powder
1 tablespoon dried oregano
200 g (7 oz) can of sweetcorn, drained
salt and pepper

To serve
steamed rice
soured cream
grated Cheddar cheese
lime wedges

1. Pop the sweet potato into a microwave-safe bowl, then cover and cook for 8 minutes on full power.

---

2. Add the chorizo, beans, tomatoes, spices, herbs and sweetcorn, then season with salt and pepper. Stir well, then cover again and cook for another 7 minutes.

---

3. Serve on a bed of steamed rice along with some soured cream, grated Cheddar and lime wedges, and garnished with extra smoked paprika.

17 MINS

 5 MINS

I first tried this dish while on holiday many years ago in Miami. I know we are not supposed to mix cuisines, but this was so good I've been cooking and eating it ever since. You can buy Cajun seasoning in the vast majority of supermarkets up and down the country. It's a great staple to have in your store cupboard, to inject loads of flavour into your dishes. Frozen prawns can also be a life-saver, as they defrost really quickly, so if you are in a bind they are ready to go in no time at all. Did you know you can also cook linguine in the microwave? Just check out my Pasta in the Microwave recipe (see page 142).

CAJUN-STYLE PRAWN LINGUINE

SERVES 4

280 g (10 oz) dried linguine
1 tablespoon olive oil
1 heaped teaspoon
    garlic paste
1 heaped tablespoon
    tomato purée
1 tablespoon Cajun
    seasoning
½ teaspoon smoked paprika
50 g (1¾ oz) chorizo,
    finely chopped
200 g (7 oz) frozen raw
    prawns, defrosted
100 g (3½ oz) cherry
    tomatoes, halved
100 g (3½ oz)
    mascarpone cheese
salt and pepper
finely grated Parmesan
    cheese, to serve

1. Cook the pasta according to the packet instructions (or see recipe introduction).

2. Meanwhile, pop the oil, garlic paste, tomato purée, spices and chorizo into a large microwave-safe bowl, season with salt and pepper, then stir well, cover and cook on full power for 2 minutes.

3. Add the prawns, tomatoes and mascarpone, then cook for a further 3 minutes, stirring halfway through.

4. Drain the pasta, but reserve some of the cooking liquid. Stir the pasta through the sauce, then add enough of the reserved cooking liquid until the sauce coats the linguine. Serve immediately sprinkled with Parmesan and extra black pepper.

LIGHTER BITES

Food doesn't always have to be heavy. I know it's nice to have a sleep on the sofa after putting back a gigantic Sunday roast, but I reserve that feeling for one day only, as we all should: Christmas Day. I believe the food we eat, the food that we use to fuel our energy levels for our busy days, should be nice and light. We want the sort of dishes that perk us up, ready to face whatever should come at us in the 24 hours ahead, not slow us down. There are other times, of course, when you just want to fill that gap between meals, or you fancy something a little bit lighter to eat. Either way, the recipes in this chapter exactly fit the bill. Here, you'll find microwave Popcorn Three Ways, with different flavourings – a really nice snack when you're feeling peckish – as well as my Speedy Red Lentil Dal, which is slightly more substantial, but still really nice and light, and even a salad or two. Many of these meals can be eaten for breakfast, brunch, lunch or dinner, so if you're looking for recipes that suit any time of the day, this is the place for you.

10 MINS

 4 MINS

 VEGETARIAN

'The' dish most Brits grew up on and definitely a meal that the rest of the world can't get their head around. This is the first thing that I cook after I get back from travelling, it just screams 'home' to me. The addition of Cheddar cheese might sound strange, but for me it's essential. You could add a perfectly poached egg on the side to make this a delicious weekend breakfast: try my microwave poached eggs (see page 20).

BEST-EVER SMOKY BEANS ON TOAST

SERVES 2

50 g (1¾ oz) chorizo, very finely chopped
1 teaspoon onion granules
½ teaspoon garlic granules
1 teaspoon smoked paprika
400 g (14 oz) can of cannellini beans, drained
1 heaped tablespoon tomato purée
1 tablespoon soft brown sugar
70 ml (2½ fl oz) boiling water
4 slices of sourdough bread
butter, for the bread
salt and pepper

To serve
Cheddar cheese, grated
chilli flakes

1. Pop the chorizo into a large microwave-safe bowl and add the onion and garlic granules, the smoked paprika, beans, tomato purée, sugar and measured boiling water. Stir to combine, then cover and cook on full power for 4 minutes, stirring halfway through. Season well with salt and pepper.

2. Meanwhile, toast the bread and spread it with butter.

3. Pile the beans on the buttered toast and sprinkle over the grated Cheddar, chilli flakes and extra black pepper to serve.

10 MINS

 16 MINS

 VEGETARIAN

I just had to do something with all those red lentils I bought during the lockdowns, so this was a solution I created that is cooked in the microwave. This deeply comforting spiced lentil dish is totally delicious and best served with a dollop of cooling yogurt, a scattering of nigella seeds and some warmed chapatis.

SPEEDY RED LENTIL DAL

SERVES 4

———

140 g (5 oz) dried red lentils
1 heaped tablespoon
   korma paste
1 heaped teaspoon
   garam masala
400 g (14 oz) can of
   chopped tomatoes
1 heaped teaspoon garlic
   and ginger paste
300 ml (½ pint) boiling
   vegetable stock
salt and pepper

To serve
1 teaspoon nigella seeds
natural yogurt
sliced green chilli
warmed chapatis

1. Place the lentils in a sieve and wash in plenty of cold water until the water runs clear.

———

2. Pop the lentils into a large microwave-safe bowl, then add the korma paste, garam masala, tomatoes, garlic and ginger paste and finally the stock.

———

3. Stir well, cover with clingfilm and cook on full power for 16 minutes, stirring halfway through.

———

4. Season with salt and pepper, then serve with a sprinkle of nigella seeds, a dollop of yogurt and some green chilli for heat, with warmed chapatis on the side.

———

7 MINS

 3½ MINS

This is a fantastic recipe for using up those little odds and ends left in the refrigerator. I don't know why, but I always seem to have an odd slice of ham, a little nugget of cheese and a few tomatoes, so when I do, this is what I make. This is just the ticket to fill a gap.

FRITTATA FOR ONE

SERVES 1

———

15 g (½ oz) butter
2 eggs, lightly beaten
4 cherry tomatoes, chopped
1 slice of ham, chopped
20 g (¾ oz) Cheddar
    cheese, grated
salt and pepper

1. Pop the butter into a microwave-safe bowl, then heat on full power for 1 minute until melted.

———

2. Add the rest of the ingredients, then whisk together with a pinch of salt and pepper.

———

3. Cover and cook for 2½ minutes, then leave to stand for 1 minute before eating straight away.

———

10 MINS

 4½ MINS

 VEGETARIAN

Anything on toast is heaven, right? And in this recipe, I've topped it with some of my favourite flavour combinations: mushrooms, cream, garlic and cheese. You can't get much better than that! A delicious lunch: sorted.

CREAMY MUSHROOMS ON TOAST

SERVES 1

———

100 g (3½ oz) chestnut
  mushrooms, sliced
15 g (½ oz) butter, plus
  more for the bread
½ teaspoon onion granules
½ teaspoon garlic paste
1 teaspoon cornflour
40 ml (1½ fl oz) double cream
20 g (¾ oz) Parmesan
  cheese, finely grated,
  plus more to serve
1 thick slice of sourdough
  bread
butter, for the bread
1 tablespoon chopped chives
salt and pepper
handful of rocket, to serve

1. Place the mushrooms, butter, onion granules and garlic paste into a medium-sized microwave-safe bowl, cover and cook on full power for 3 minutes.

———

2. Meanwhile, in a cup, mix the cornflour with 1 tablespoon of water to a smooth paste.

———

3. Stir the mushrooms, then add the cornflour paste, cream and Parmesan, cover again and return to the microwave to cook for a further 90 seconds. Season with salt and lots of pepper.

———

4. While that's happening, toast the bread and spread it with the butter.

———

5. Spoon the mushrooms on the hot buttered toast, then sprinkle over the chives and a little more Parmesan. Season to taste and serve with a handful of rocket on the side.

———

10 MINS

 3 MINS

 VEGETARIAN

This recipe is the definition of summer on a plate. The vegetables are cooked to perfection in the microwave and then served up on a sharing plate ready for you to tuck in. Burrata cheese has to be up there as one of my favourite ingredients that has hit the supermarket shelves in recent years: just think mozzarella cheese but a million times better! So creamy and delicious, and a perfect partner for these vegetables.

ZESTY ASPARAGUS & PEAS WITH BURRATA

SERVES 2

1 bunch of asparagus
100 g (3½ oz) frozen
 peas, defrosted
100 g (3½ oz) sugar snaps,
 sliced lengthways
150 g (5½ oz) ball of burrata
50 g (1¾ oz) toasted
 hazelnuts

For the dressing
finely grated zest and juice
 of ½ lemon
2 tablespoons extra virgin
 olive oil, plus more to serve
½ teaspoon wholegrain
 mustard
1 teaspoon honey
salt and pepper

1. Take each asparagus spear and bend it: it will snap at the place where it becomes tough. Discard these pieces, or use them to make soup another time. Cut the asparagus into bite-sized pieces.

2. Place the asparagus, peas and sugar snaps into a microwave-safe bowl, then cover and cook on full power for 3 minutes.

3. Meanwhile, whisk together the dressing ingredients, then season with a touch of salt and pepper.

4. Pour the dressing over the vegetables, then mix well.

5. Tip on to a serving plate, then add the ball of burrata, scatter over the hazelnuts and finish with some pepper and a drizzle of olive oil.

15 MINS

 3½ MINS

 VEGETARIAN

A hearty but light vegetarian dish that will set your taste buds on fire. Chickpeas are such a versatile ingredient, so they are always in my store cupboard. This lightning-quick curry works perfectly as a topping for warm naans, with a lovely creamy raita to cut through the spice.

SPICY CHICKPEA NAANS

SERVES 2

400 g (14 oz) can of
   chickpeas, drained
1 tablespoon tomato purée
1 tablespoon korma paste
150 ml (¼ pint) boiling
   vegetable stock
1 teaspoon sugar
2 naans
salt and pepper

For the mint raita
¼ cucumber
100 ml (3½ fl oz)
   natural yogurt
1 tablespoon mint sauce
   from a jar
½ teaspoon sugar

To serve
Kachumber Salad
   (see page 134)
coriander leaves
chopped green chilli

1. To make the mint raita, slice the cucumber section lengthways, then use a teaspoon to scoop out the seeds from each half (discard those). Finely chop the cucumber. Combine all the ingredients in a small bowl and set aside while you make the rest of the meal.

——

2. Pop the chickpeas, tomato purée, korma paste, boiling stock and sugar into a medium-sized microwave-safe bowl, along with a pinch of salt and pepper, and mix well. Cover and cook on full power for 3 minutes, stirring halfway through.

——

3. Warm the naans in the microwave for 20 seconds, then top with the chickpea curry. Sprinkle the kachumber salad on top, garnish with coriander leaves and serve with the mint raita and chopped green chilli on the side.

——

8 MINS

 4 MINS

 VEGETARIAN

We all love chips and dips, right? Well, nothing could be easier than this spicy nacho cheese dip, just perfect for scooping up with tortilla chips of your choice. It's the perfect snack for sharing with friends and family at a get-together, or when you're sitting down with mates to watch the big game.

JALAPEÑO & CHEESE NACHO DIP

SERVES 4

1 tablespoon cornflour
170 g (6 oz) can of
   evaporated milk
100 g (3½ oz) Mexicana
   cheese, grated
1 fresh jalapeño chilli,
   finely chopped
½ teaspoon smoked paprika
salt and pepper
tortilla chips, to serve

1. In a cup, mix the cornflour with 1 tablespoon of cold water to a smooth paste. Pour the evaporated milk into a microwave-safe bowl, mix it with the cornflour paste and cook on full power for 3 minutes.

2. Add the cheese, jalapeño and paprika, then stir to combine. Cook for a further 1 minute, then stir well until the cheese has melted. Season with salt and pepper to taste.

3. Serve with tortilla chips for dipping.

5 MINS

 5½ MINS

 VEGETARIAN

Popcorn is the ultimate snack. You might also be surprised how easy it is to cook at home using your trusty microwave. I've given three of my best flavour options here, but feel free to experiment with your favourite flavours. Just use the basic method below and get creative.

POPCORN THREE WAYS

EACH SERVES 1

40 g (1½ oz) popping
 corn kernels

For truffle popcorn
20 g (¾ oz) salted butter
2–3 drops of truffle oil
small pinch of salt

For curried popcorn
20 g (¾ oz) salted butter
¼ teaspoon smoked paprika
¼ teaspoon ground cumin
¼ teaspoon chilli powder

For salted honey popcorn
20 g (¾ oz) salted butter
2 tablespoons honey
small pinch of salt, or to taste

1. Measure out the kernels into a large microwave-safe bowl, place a microwave-safe plate on top, then cook on full power for 5 minutes until popped.

2. Throw in the butter and the rest of the chosen flavourings, then microwave for a further 30 seconds until the butter has melted.

3. Toss together so the popcorn gets an even coating of all the flavourings, then tip into a serving bowl, discarding any kernels that haven't popped.

10 MINS

 3 MINS

As you can probably tell, smoky paprika-rich chorizo is one of my favourite flavours. We all have staples in our refrigerator and pantry and chorizo is one of mine. It is a fantastic ingredient; it's so easy just to pull it out and use it to knock up something super tasty. This time, combining it with a humble can of beans makes a delicious warm summer salad. I hope you enjoy it as much as I do.

WARM CHORIZO & BEAN SALAD

SERVES 2

2 tablespoons olive oil
1 teaspoon garlic paste
½ teaspoon smoked paprika
60 g (2¼ oz) chorizo,
    finely sliced
400 g (14 oz) can of cannellini
    beans, drained
1 teaspoon sherry vinegar
1 teaspoon wholegrain
    mustard
1 teaspoon honey
60 g (2¼ oz) bag of
    lamb's lettuce
80 g (2¾ oz) cherry
    tomatoes, halved
¼ red onion, finely sliced
salt and pepper

1. Pop the oil, garlic paste, paprika, chorizo, cannellini beans, vinegar, mustard and honey into a large microwave-safe bowl, add a pinch of salt and pepper, then cover and cook on full power for 3 minutes.

———

2. Leave to stand for 2 minutes.

———

3. Plate up the lettuce, tomatoes and onion, then gently toss through the bean and chorizo mixture to coat.

———

10 MINS

 8 MINS

Cod is a delicious fish to eat and it can stand up to strong, punchy ingredients, so combining it with this flavour-packed Spanish-inspired tomato stew is an absolute winner. The fish cooks on top of the sauce and it's all done in one dish, so it also saves on the washing up. Serve this with crispy patatas bravas-style potatoes for the win.

SPANISH-STYLE COD & SMOKY TOMATO STEW

SERVES 4

2 roasted peppers from
  a jar, finely sliced
400 g (14 oz) can of
  chopped tomatoes
1 heaped teaspoon
  smoked paprika
1 tablespoon sherry vinegar
1 heaped teaspoon sugar
4 small skinless cod fillets,
  total weight about
  300 g (10½ oz)
50 g (1¾ oz) pitted black
  olives, halved
2 tablespoons chopped
  parsley leaves
½ teaspoon chilli flakes
salt and pepper

To serve
crusty bread
lemon wedges

1. Place the peppers, chopped tomatoes, paprika, vinegar and sugar into a microwave-safe baking dish measuring about 24 × 18 cm (9½ × 7 inches), add a pinch of salt and pepper, then mix well, cover and cook on full power for 3 minutes.

——

2. Stir well, then gently place on the cod fillets, cover again and cook for a further 5 minutes.

——

3. Leave to stand for 2 minutes, then scatter over the olives, parsley and chilli flakes and serve with crusty bread and lemon wedges.

——

ON THE SIDE

Side dishes are not only there to work with the main element of a meal, sometimes they can be the star of the show. Many sausages have had their thunder stolen by a mound of world-beating creamy Champ Mashed Potatoes. Just as many drab puddings have been rescued by a generous drizzle of beautiful Vanilla Custard. You know what I'm saying: side dishes can really make a meal into something spectacular.

There's also a very practical side to this chapter. The fact that you're able to cook staples such as pasta and jacket potatoes in your microwave – without the need of a big pot of boiling water or an energy-consuming hot oven – can make your life so much easier, and your bills that bit smaller.

18 MINS

 12 MINS

 VEGETARIAN

Who doesn't love a potato salad in the summer? It's the perfect side dish to go alongside a barbecue, when you're enjoying a sunny day in the garden with friends and family. I'm taking inspiration here from a trip I took to Greece a few years ago, when I fell in love with Greek salad. It's incredible how such a simple flavour combination can be so delicious and just goes to show that great food doesn't have to be complicated.

GREEK-STYLE POTATO SALAD

SERVES 4

---

700 g (1 lb 9 oz) new
   potatoes, halved
100 g (3½ oz) feta
   cheese, crumbled
finely grated zest and
   juice of ½ lemon
2 tablespoons mayonnaise
½ red onion, chopped
100 g (3½ oz) cherry
   tomatoes, halved
salt and pepper

To serve
chopped cucumber
black olives

1. Pop the new potatoes into a microwave-safe bowl. Cover and cook for 12 minutes on full power, stirring halfway through. Leave to cool.

---

2. Stir through the feta, lemon zest and juice, mayonnaise, red onion and tomatoes. Gently mix until the potatoes are coated.

---

3. Check the seasoning, adding salt and pepper if required – though you may not need it as the feta is quite salty – and serve scattered with chopped cucumber and accompanied by black olives.

5 MINS

 10 MINS

 VEGETARIAN

I remember vividly going to listen to one of my favourite chefs, Heston Blumenthal, give a talk in my home city of Bristol. If you're familiar with Heston's work, you will know he's a chef with a scientist's brain. The way he spoke about food completely changed my view point. Among other things, he talked about how much flavour is lost to the water when you boil any ingredient. Simple ingredients such as carrots don't taste like carrots any more because of this. My microwave-glazed carrots were born from that talk and I've never cooked them differently since.

ORANGE & HONEY GLAZED CARROTS

SERVES 4

400 g (14 oz) baby carrots, peeled
juice of ½ orange
30 g (1 oz) unsalted butter
1 teaspoon honey
½ teaspoon dried thyme
salt and pepper

1. Top the carrots, then pop them into a microwave-safe baking dish measuring about 24 × 18 cm (9½ × 7 inches).

2. Add the orange juice, butter, honey and finally the dried thyme. Season with salt and pepper, then cover and cook on full power for 10 minutes, shaking halfway through.

3. Leave to stand for 2 minutes before serving.

15 MINS

 4 MINS

 VEGETARIAN

For me, the poppadums and the chutney tray at my local Indian restaurant are usually my favourite part of the meal. I just love the combination of crispy poppadum and the balance of the toppings, usually mint raita, sticky mango chutney and sharp kachumber salad. I bet you didn't know that you can cook poppadums in your microwave... and using a fraction of the oil, too.

CRISPY POPPADUMS WITH KACHUMBER SALAD

SERVES 4
———

4 uncooked poppadums
2 teaspoons vegetable oil

For the kachumber salad
2 tomatoes, chopped
½ red onion, chopped
¼ cucumber, deseeded
    (see page 120) and chopped
½ teaspoon sugar
juice of ½ lemon
salt and pepper

To serve (optional)
Mint Raita (see page 120)
mango chutney

1. To make the kachumber salad, combine all the ingredients in a bowl with some salt and pepper, then leave to stand for 10 minutes before serving.

———

2. Brush both sides of a poppadum with a little oil, then place on a sheet of kitchen paper and set on a microwave-safe plate.

———

3. Cook one poppadum at a time, on full power, for 1 minute, until crisp.

———

4. Serve the poppadums with the kachumber salad, along with some mint raita and mango chutney, if liked.

———

5 MINS

 4 MINS

VEGETARIAN

Cauliflower rice was huge on the food scene a few years ago because it is absolutely perfect for people who are following a low-carb diet. I enjoy it because it's super-tasty and a great way of adding extra vegetables into your diet. You can actually buy pouches of microwaveable cauliflower rice in the supermarkets now... but why would you, when it's so easy to make at home? This works perfectly with my Butter Chicken Curry (see page 94).

STEAMED CAULIFLOWER RICE

SERVES 4

1 large cauliflower
4 teaspoons water
salt and pepper

1. To make the cauliflower rice, either grate the cauliflower, or pop it into a food processor and pulse-blend until it resembles rice.

2. Tip the cauliflower into a large microwave-safe bowl, then add the measured water and a good pinch of salt and pepper, cover tightly with clingfilm, poke a few holes in the top and cook on full power for 4 minutes.

Tip

You can freeze the raw cauliflower rice in portions, then, when you want to eat it, microwave as above from frozen for 6 minutes, stirring halfway through.

10 MINS

 16 MINS

 VEGETARIAN

This side dish will always have its place on the elite tier when it comes to vegetables to eat with a Sunday lunch. Swede and carrot is such a fantastic combination, but what elevates this is the addition of lots of white pepper; it really does take it to the next level. To make the vegetables easier to mash, I pulse-blend them in a food processor first.

PEPPERY SWEDE & CARROT MASH

SERVES 4

---

300 g (10½ oz) carrots, peeled and chopped
300 g (10½ oz) swede, peeled and chopped the same size as the carrots
50 ml (1¾ oz) boiling vegetable stock, made with 1 stock pot
30 g (1 oz) butter
½ teaspoon ground white pepper
salt

1. Place the carrots and swede into a large microwave-safe bowl, then pour in the stock. Cover and cook for 16 minutes on full power, stirring halfway through.

---

2. Leave to stand for a couple of minutes, then mash (see recipe introduction), with the butter, some salt and the generous amount of white pepper.

Tip

Make sure to cut the vegetables to the same size, as this ensures they will cook evenly.

12 MINS

 14 MINS

 VEGETARIAN

The side dish of 'Champ' ions! (Sorry...) Mashed potatoes are lush at the best of times, but the addition of spring onions takes them to a new level. Cooking the spuds in the microwave, rather than boiling them, means you keep much more of the real potato flavour in this side dish.

CHAMP MASHED POTATOES

SERVES 4
———

800 g (1 lb 12 oz) potatoes, peeled and cut into small cubes
150 ml (¼ pint) milk
40 g (1½ oz) unsalted butter
6 spring onions, sliced
salt and pepper

1. Pop the potatoes into a microwave-safe bowl, cover and cook on full power for 14 minutes, shaking halfway through.
———

2. Pour in the milk, then add the butter and a good pinch of salt and pepper.
———

3. Cover again and cook for a further 2 minutes. Mash until smooth, then stir through the spring onions.
———

20 MINS

 18 MINS

Jacket potatoes are something that we all tend to use a microwave for, on a regular basis. It cuts the cooking time down hugely and saves on those costly oven energy bills. You can zap them until they cook through, then pop them into the oven or air fryer to crisp up that skin. However, these loaded potato skins are so delicious that you will never again cook your spuds any other way.

LOADED POTATO SKINS

SERVES 2

2 streaky bacon rashers
2 large baking potatoes, about 250 g (9 oz) each
1 teaspoon vegetable oil
20 g (¾ oz) butter
2 tablespoons soured cream, plus more to serve
80 g (2¾ oz) Cheddar cheese, grated
3 spring onions, finely sliced
salt and pepper
handful of rocket, to serve

Tip

Whenever you cook jacket potatoes in the microwave, make sure to prick the skins, to stop them bursting during cooking.

1. Place the bacon on a microwave-safe plate, lightly cover with a sheet of kitchen paper and microwave on full power for 1 minute. Turn each rasher over, cover with the kitchen paper again, then cook for a further 1 minute. Leave to cool, then chop into a bacon 'crumb'.

2. Wash and dry the potatoes, then rub them with the oil and prick all over with a fork. Place a sheet of kitchen paper on a microwave-safe plate, then pop the potatoes on top. Cook on full power for 7 minutes, turn each potato over, then cook for a further 7 minutes. Leave to stand for 2 minutes.

3. Cut the potatoes in half lengthways, then spoon out the insides into a bowl. Add the butter, soured cream and half the Cheddar, then season with salt and pepper. Mash together until fluffy, then stir through most of the bacon and spring onions, reserving some to serve. Mix until fully incorporated.

4. Spoon the filling back into the skins, then sprinkle over the remaining cheese. Return to the microwave and cook for a further 2 minutes. Sprinkle over the reserved spring onions and bacon and serve with an extra dollop of soured cream and a handful of rocket on the side.

2 MINS

 14 MINS

 VEGETARIAN

Pasta is such an important staple ingredient in the store cupboard; I would go so far as to suggest that the vast majority of households in the UK have some form of pasta ready and waiting in the kitchen at all times. For a whole pasta feast made in the microwave, try my Spaghetti Amatriciana, with its beautiful tomato sauce, or my classic Spaghetti Carbonara (see pages 74 and 80). For those recipes, and more, this is the recipe you will need to knock up pasta in your microwave.

PASTA IN THE MICROWAVE

SERVES 1

———

90 g (3¼ oz) pasta
  of your choice
1 teaspoon salt

1. Tip the pasta into a microwave-safe bowl or dish, then pour in boiling water and add the salt, making sure the pasta is completely covered with water.

2. Cover and cook on full power for 3 minutes longer than the suggested cooking time on the packet. For example, if the packet states to cook for 11 minutes, cook in the microwave for 14 minutes.

3. Drain, then serve with your favourite sauce.

———

Tip

If using spaghetti, find a suitable dish that allows you to fit it in within a single layer, or just snap the pasta in half to fit inside a smaller one.

10 MINS

 1½ MINS

 VEGETARIAN

If you're looking to add a touch of crunch and texture to a soup, then these are absolutely delicious. I particularly love them with my Minted Pea Soup (see page 36).

PARMESAN CRISPS

MAKES 2 LARGE CRISPS

30 g (1 oz) Parmesan
    cheese, finely grated
a few twists of freshly
    cracked black pepper

1. Line a microwave-safe plate with a sheet of baking parchment. Gently scatter half the Parmesan on to the parchment and shape into a circle, then repeat with the second lot of cheese. Sprinkle over some black pepper.

2. Microwave on full power for 90 seconds, then leave to cool, before carefully removing the crisps from the parchment.

3 MINS

 2 MINS

 VEGETARIAN

The ultimate sauce for a dessert, enjoyed by all generations on dishes such as steamed pudding, or my Apple & Berry Crumble Pot (see page 166). A classic custard takes a lot of beating. I was actually taught how to make custard by culinary legend Michel Roux Jr. It was a nerve-wracking experience, but it gave me the foundation to be able to create this super-simple and easy microwave version for you to enjoy.

VANILLA CUSTARD

SERVES 4

---

3 egg yolks
30 g (1 oz) caster sugar
1 teaspoon vanilla extract
15 g (½ oz) cornflour
180 ml (6 fl oz) whole milk

1. Whisk together all the ingredients in a microwave-safe bowl until fully combined.

---

2. Cover with clingfilm, then cook in 30-second bursts, whisking after each one. This should take about 2 minutes.

---

3. If, after this time, the custard is not quite thick enough for you, continue to cook in 10-second bursts, whisking after every cook, until it reaches your preferred consistency.

Tip

Try adding a dash of Amaretto, or Irish liqueur, to the finished custard, for a delicious adult twist.

TIME-SAVER MEALS & CHEAT INGREDIENTS

The recipes in this chapter are designed to make your microwave-cooking life even easier, whether that is by using a time-saving shop-bought ingredient, or by employing the microwave to create speedy versions of dishes that normally take a long time.

My creamy Pea & Leek Risotto is one of the latter recipes. Traditionally, a risotto takes both time and patience to get right, adding boiling stock just a ladleful at a time while gently stirring until cooked. My microwave version takes all the hard work out of it; you stir just once during the cooking process and the results are absolutely incredible. You will never cook risotto in any other way again.

Meanwhile, ingredients such as microwave rice and fresh noodles – which you can easily buy at any supermarket – can be transformed in the microwave into a delicious meal in just minutes. Make sure to give my Ginger Chicken Udon Noodles and Prawn Nasi Goreng – a spicy Indonesian rice dish – a try.

12 MINS

 4½ MINS

 VEGETARIAN

Fondue was all the rage in the 1970s and 1980s, but let me tell you that cheese never goes out of fashion! No longer do you have the faff of cooking this dish in a pan; now it's super simple to make in your microwave and takes just minutes. Dip away with whatever you fancy: crudités such as radishes, apples and peppers, or some roasted new potatoes, of course, but make sure your choices include my favourite option: garlic bread.

CHEESE FONDUE

SERVES 4

---

150 ml (¼ pint) white wine
1 heaped teaspoon cornflour
150 g (5½ oz) Gruyère
  cheese, grated
150 g (5½ oz) Emmental
  cheese, grated
½ teaspoon garlic granules

To serve
your choice of crudités,
  such as radishes, sliced
  apples and sliced peppers
roasted new potatoes
garlic bread

1. Pour the wine into a large microwave-safe bowl, then cook on full power for 90 seconds. Meanwhile, in a cup, mix the cornflour with 1 tablespoon of cold water to a smooth paste.

---

2. Add both the cheeses to the hot wine with the garlic granules and cornflour paste, then stir well.

---

3. Cover and microwave in 1-minute bursts, stirring after each, until the cheese has melted and pulls into strings when you lift a spoon out. This will take about 3 minutes. Serve straight away with your choice of crudités, roasted new potatoes and garlic bread.

15 MINS

 11 MINS

 VEGETARIAN

I'm betting you only ever griddle or barbecue halloumi cheese, or 'squeaky cheese', as my daughter Indie calls it. Well, I'm going to show you another way to enjoy this traditional Cypriot delicacy, within this flavour-packed stew. The cheese has a high melting point, which not only makes it perfect for cooking over the fierce heat of a barbecue, but also in the fierce focussed heat of a microwave. I like to serve this with rice and garlic bread.

HALLOUMI & RED PEPPER STEW

SERVES 4
———

1 small onion, finely chopped
1 teaspoon garlic paste
1 tablespoon olive oil
400 g (14 oz) can of
    chopped tomatoes
1 roasted red pepper
    from a jar, sliced
    (about 100 g/3½ oz)
400 g (14 oz) can of cannellini
    beans, drained
1 tablespoon rose harissa
1 teaspoon sugar
1 vegetable stock pot
225 g (8 oz) pack of
    halloumi cheese, cut
    into bite-sized cubes
salt and pepper

To serve
steamed rice
chopped parsley leaves
chilli flakes
garlic bread (optional)

1. Pop the onion, garlic paste and oil into a large microwave-safe bowl, then stir well, cover and cook on full power for 3 minutes.

———

2. Add the tomatoes, pepper, beans, harissa, sugar and stock pot. Stir, then cover again and cook for 5 minutes.

———

3. Finally, add the halloumi and cook for 3 minutes. Check the seasoning: you may not need to add too much salt, as halloumi is quite salty.

———

4. Leave to stand for 2 minutes, then portion into bowls on a bed of steamed rice. Scatter with chopped parsley and chilli flakes and serve with some garlic bread, if liked.

———

Tip

Using a stock pot in a recipe allows you to add extra flavour without any additional liquid.

10 MINS

 7 MINS

 VEGETARIAN

Sometimes you need to use up the ingredients you have in your store cupboard and, often, that's when you come up with ingenious meal ideas. Don't get me wrong: a beautiful authentic biryani is an incredible dish, but when you haven't got some of the specialized ingredients for that in the house and you just need to chuck something together, you'll go a long way to find something better than this recipe.

STORE CUPBOARD CHICKPEA BIRYANI

SERVES 2

400 g (14 oz) can
   of chickpeas
1 red pepper, deseeded
   and chopped
1 teaspoon garlic and
   ginger paste
1 heaped tablespoon
   korma paste
1 heaped tablespoon
   tomato purée
100 ml (3½ fl oz) boiling
   vegetable stock
½ teaspoon sugar,
   or to taste
3½ tablespoons
   natural yogurt
2 × 250 g (9 oz) pouches of
   microwave basmati rice
30 g (1 oz) dried cranberries
handful of coriander leaves,
   chopped
salt and pepper

1. Tip the chickpeas into a microwave-safe bowl and stir in the pepper, garlic and ginger paste, korma paste, tomato purée and the boiling stock.

2. Season with salt and pepper, then cover and cook for 5 minutes on full power.

3. Once cooked, stir through the sugar and yogurt, then sprinkle over the rice, cover again and cook for a further 2 minutes.

4. Before serving, give the rice a gentle stir and scatter over the dried cranberries and coriander.

12 MINS

11 MINS

Who doesn't love a hearty bowl of stew? This is so packed full of flavour and is absolutely nothing like your nan used to make... unless your nan was Italian. Stews are a fantastic way to put an easy meal on the table, plus you can use store cupboard ingredients and leftovers to bulk them out. I love to use cavolo nero, aka black cabbage, in this recipe, but if you can't find it, use Savoy cabbage instead.

TUSCAN-STYLE BEAN STEW

SERVES 2

100 g (3½ oz) smoked bacon lardons
1 tablespoon olive oil
1 onion, finely chopped
1 heaped teaspoon garlic paste
400 g (14 oz) can of cannellini beans, drained
400 g (14 oz) can of black beans, drained
400 g (14 oz) can of chopped tomatoes
1 tablespoon dried oregano
60 g (2¼ oz) cabbage leaves, shredded (see recipe introduction)
150 ml (¼ pint) vegetable stock, made from a stock pot
salt and pepper
crusty bread, to serve
finely grated Parmesan cheese, to garnish

1. Pop the bacon, oil, onion and garlic paste into a large microwave-safe bowl, then cover with a sheet of kitchen paper and cook on full power for 3 minutes.

2. Add both types of beans, the tomatoes, oregano, cabbage and stock, season with salt and pepper, then stir well. Cover and cook for a further 8 minutes, stirring halfway through.

3. Portion into bowls, then grate over some Parmesan and serve with crusty bread on the side.

10 MINS

 16 MINS

 VEGETARIAN

A risotto can be a tricky and time-consuming dish to cook in the traditional way, gradually adding stock until it has been absorbed and constantly stirring to release the creamy starch that comes from arborio rice. My microwave version is a game changer. It's so simple to make and you can use whatever vegetables are in season, so why not try some asparagus in spring, spinach in summer or even my Butternut Squash & Blue Cheese Risotto (see page 76) in the autumn?

PEA & LEEK RISOTTO

SERVES 2

---

30 g (1 oz) unsalted butter, plus 30 g (1 oz)

1 small leek (about 100 g/ 3½ oz), shredded

1 teaspoon garlic paste

150 g (5½ oz) arborio rice

500 ml (18 fl oz) boiling vegetable stock

100 g (3½ oz) frozen peas

30 g (1 oz) Parmesan cheese, finely grated

30 g (1 oz) unsalted butter

1. Pop the 30 g (1 oz) of butter, the leek and garlic paste into a microwave-safe bowl, then cook on full power for 2 minutes.

---

2. Stir in the rice, making sure it has a good coating of the butter. Pour in half the stock, then stir well, cover and cook on full power for 7 minutes.

---

3. Add the remaining stock and the peas (they can go in while frozen), stir, cover again and cook for a further 7 minutes.

---

4. Leave to stand for 2 minutes, then fold through the Parmesan and remaining 30 g (1 oz) of butter.

---

12 MINS

 6 MINS

 VEGETARIAN

Make the most of any chicken leftovers with this incredible chicken soup. I was always taught never to waste food, so on those occasions we had a roast chicken, it was my job to make sure that every scrap of meat was picked from the carcass. This sometimes went into a sandwich, but more often than not it ended up in soup. A little leftover meat goes a long way in this recipe, not only in flavour but texture, too.

EGG DROP SOUP

SERVES 2

200 g (7 oz) cooked chicken, shredded
600 ml (1 pint) chicken stock
1 tablespoon fish sauce
198 g (7 oz) can of sweetcorn, drained
4 spring onions, finely chopped
1 tablespoon cornflour
2 eggs
salt and white pepper
chilli flakes, to garnish

1. Place the chicken in a large microwave-safe bowl, then pour in the chicken stock and fish sauce, tip in the sweetcorn and add the white part of the spring onions (reserve the green parts). Cover and cook on full power for 3 minutes.

2. Meanwhile, in a cup, mix the cornflour with 1 tablespoon of water together to a smooth paste. Add this to the broth, stirring well. Pop back into the microwave for a further 3 minutes.

3. Lightly beat the eggs with 2 tablespoons of water in a jug. Slowly pour this into the hot cooked broth, stirring as you go, so the eggs become fine ribbons within the soup.

4. Season well with salt and white pepper and portion into bowls. Scatter with the reserved green spring onions and some chilli flakes and serve.

7 MINS

 3 MINS

 VEGETARIAN

If you like your eggs, this is a recipe you need to try. Chinese steamed eggs have the most incredible silken texture, as well as being jam-packed with flavour. I top this protein-packed lunch with sliced spring onions for texture and loads of smoky Chiu Chow chilli oil, which you can buy in most supermarkets now. If you can't find it, it will definitely be stocked online, or in your local Asian supermarket.

CHINESE-STYLE STEAMED EGGS

SERVES 1

2 eggs
140 ml (5 fl oz) boiling
   chicken stock
1 tablespoon fish sauce
1 teaspoon Chiu Chow
   chilli oil
2 spring onions,
   finely sliced
1 teaspoon black
   sesame seeds

1. Crack the eggs into a microwave-safe serving bowl, then pour in the boiling stock and fish sauce.

2. Whisk together, then cover and cook on full power for 3 minutes.

3. Leave to stand for 2 minutes, then add as much crispy chilli oil as you can handle and serve with a scattering of spring onions and sesame seeds.

10 MINS

 7½ MINS

I've been fortunate enough to travel to Germany a few times in my life, starting with a school trip. I think it was at that point that I fell in love with the place and its food. One of the first things I remember trying as a 13-year-old was curry wurst. It was delicious: a frankfurter sausage smothered in a sweet and spicy curry ketchup. Yes, you can serve these in a roll, but I prefer mine classic German-style, sliced into rounds and smothered in the spicy ketchup, with fries on the side.

CURRY WURST

SERVES 4

1 onion, finely chopped
1 teaspoon garlic paste
1 teaspoon vegetable oil
100 ml (3½ fl oz)
    tomato ketchup
1 heaped teaspoon mild
    curry powder
1 teaspoon sweet paprika
3 tablespoons
    Worcestershire sauce
2 tablespoons cider vinegar
1 tablespoon sugar
4 jumbo frankfurter-style
    hot dogs
salt and pepper

Tip

Microwave on high for 90 seconds for 1 frankfurter. When cooking more than 1 hot dog, add an additional 20 seconds per sausage.

1. Pop the onion, garlic paste and oil into a microwave-safe bowl, cover and microwave on full power for 3 minutes.

2. Add the ketchup, spices, Worcestershire sauce, vinegar, sugar and a pinch of salt and pepper. Cover again and cook for a further 2 minutes.

3. Transfer the mixture to a small food processor and blitz the sauce until smooth.

4. Prick each frankfurter a few times with a sharp knife, to stop them bursting. Place on a microwave-safe plate and cover with a damp sheet of kitchen paper. Cook on full power for 2½ minutes. Use a probe thermometer to check the internal temperature has reached at least 75°C (167°F).

5. Slice the frankfurters and stir them into the sauce to serve.

10 MINS

 7 MINS

I can't take credit for the flavour combinations in this recipe; I was inspired by a trip to a well-known Japanese restaurant chain... All I can say is that it was a really tasty dish and I wanted to make it work in the microwave. You won't believe how simple this recipe is: the chicken sauce and noodles cook in the same dish and you just add as much chilli as you can handle. But the kicker for me is the pickled ginger, which really adds another level to these noodles.

GINGER CHICKEN UDON NOODLES

SERVES 2

2 skinless boneless
   chicken thighs, cut
   into bite-sized pieces
2 tablespoons soy sauce
2 tablespoons sweet
   chilli sauce
1 heaped teaspoon garlic
   and ginger paste
80 g (2¾ oz) sugar snaps,
   sliced lengthways
2 × 150 g (5½ oz) ready-
   to-wok udon noodles
   (I used Amoy)
4 spring onions, sliced
1 red chilli, finely sliced
1 tablespoon shredded
   pickled ginger (try
   to find pink ginger)

1. Place the chicken in a microwave-safe baking dish measuring about 24 × 18 cm (9½ × 7 inches), ensuring the chicken is in an even layer.

2. Pour in the soy sauce, sweet chilli sauce and garlic and ginger paste, mix well, then cover and cook on full power for 4 minutes.

3. Add the sugar snaps and noodles, then cover again and cook for a further 3 minutes. Leave to stand for 2 minutes, then stir well to combine all the ingredients.

4. Portion into serving bowls, then scatter with the spring onions, red chilli and shredded pickled ginger.

8 MINS

 3 MINS

A few years ago, I was lucky enough to work on cruise ships. It was an incredible experience and I got to see some beautiful places. A lot of the chefs on board were Indonesian and, at lunch, they loved to showcase their own food. The nasi goreng which was served up to the guests on board was simply divine. This microwave version definitely packs a punch. If you can find sambal oelek – a hot red chilli paste – in your local Asian supermarket, it goes great with this dish, especially if you like a chilli kick.

PRAWN NASI GORENG

SERVES 1
———

1 × 250 g (9 oz) pouch
    of microwave rice
3 spring onions, sliced
1 teaspoon garlic paste
2 tablespoons kecap manis
1 tablespoon soy sauce
1 red chilli, deseeded
    and finely chopped
100 g (3½ oz) cooked
    prawns
1 'Fried' Egg (see page 56)
sweet chilli sauce, to serve

1. Tip the rice into a microwave-safe bowl, break it up with a fork, add the white parts of the spring onions and the garlic paste, then cover and cook for 2 minutes.

———

2. Stir, then mix through the kecap manis, soy sauce, chilli and prawns, cover again and cook for a further minute.

———

3. Scatter over the green parts of the spring onions and serve with a microwave 'fried' egg and some sweet chilli sauce.

———

SOMETHING SWEET

I thought this chapter would present the biggest challenge to me in the whole book. I'm going to let you into a little secret: probably the first dessert I ever cooked as a kid was actually made in the microwave. I remember my mum showing me how you could make a baked apple: we cored it, stuffed it with raisins, then microwaved it on full power until it was soft. I'd eat that with a nice scoop of vanilla ice cream. I automatically assumed that recipe would make it into this chapter, no problem. But, as I started to experiment with the sweet treats I was cooking in my microwave, it dawned on me that those baked apples were never going to come even close to making the final cut. What I found was that maximizing the microwave meant there was literally no limit to my creativity.

So sorry, Mum, your baked apple had to make way for my Ginger & Treacle Sponges, the legendary Salted Caramel Millionaire's Shortbread and – one of my absolute favourites – a comforting Mango & Coconut Rice Pudding.

7 MINS

 3 MINS

 VEGETARIAN

Would you believe you can make this fruit crumble in less than five minutes? That's handy, as I quite often find myself craving a sweet treat out of nowhere, and frozen berries are just the trick for making this delicious dessert in no time. I always have the usual suspects such as blueberries, blackberries, raspberries and blackcurrants in the freezer. Not only are these delicious in this crumble, but they're great for topping yogurt and for using in smoothies, so good to keep in stock.

APPLE & BERRY CRUMBLE POT

SERVES 1
—

1 Braeburn apple
   (about 80 g/2¾ oz),
   peeled and cut into
   1 cm (½ inch) cubes
80 g (2¾ oz) frozen
   summer berries
1 tablespoon honey
¼ teaspoon ground
   cinnamon
1 teaspoon cornflour
1 teaspoon unsalted butter
2 tablespoons granola
vanilla ice cream, to serve

1. Place the apple, frozen berries, honey, cinnamon and cornflour into a microwave-safe ramekin, stir, then add the knob of butter.

—

2. Cover and cook on full power for 3 minutes. Leave to stand for 1 minute, then stir gently.

—

3. Scatter over the granola, then serve with a dollop of vanilla ice cream.

—

25 MINS

 9½ MINS

 VEGETARIAN

I just adore the flavour of passion fruit; it's unique and the balance of sweetness and tartness works so well in a curd. Usually you would make a curd over a double boiler, being very careful not to scramble the eggs, but this microwave version is so easy, why wouldn't you do it this way instead? I love to serve this light and fluffy sponge with some Greek yogurt, to add a touch of creaminess.

PASSION FRUIT & LIME CURD SPONGE

SERVES 6

For the curd
4 passion fruits
juice of 1 lime
2 eggs, lightly beaten
120 g (4¼ oz) caster sugar
100 g (3½ oz) unsalted
    butter, cubed
1 heaped teaspoon cornflour

For the sponge
120 g (4¼ oz) unsalted
    butter, softened, plus
    more for the bowl
120 g (4¼ oz) caster sugar
120 g (4¼ oz) self-raising
    flour
2 tablespoons whole milk
2 eggs, lightly beaten
finely grated zest of 1 lime,
    plus more to serve

To serve
2 passion fruits
Greek yogurt

1. Start with the curd. Halve the passion fruits, then scrape out the seeds and pulp into a microwave-safe bowl. Add the lime juice, eggs, sugar, butter and cornflour.

2. Microwave in 30-second bursts. After each burst, whisk to combine the ingredients together. It should take about 3½ minutes in total for the curd to thicken (see tip, below), then pass it through a sieve and leave to cool.

3. Meanwhile, butter a 1-litre (1¾ pint) microwave-safe bowl, which is about 17 cm (6½ inches) in diameter.

4. Make the sponge by whisking together the butter, sugar, flour, milk, eggs and lime zest until light and fluffy. Transfer to the prepared bowl, cover with clingfilm, then cook on full power for 6 minutes. Leave to stand for 5 minutes.

5. Portion the sponge into bowls, then serve with the curd, passion fruits, lime zest and Greek yogurt.

Tip

If your curd hasn't thickened after the allotted cooking time, then keep cooking it in 15-second bursts until it has, making sure to whisk it after each burst.

10 MINS

 15 MINS

 VEGETARIAN

Dessert-wise, is there a better combination than apple and cinnamon? It's a flavour marriage made in heaven. This is such a simple sweet treat to make, using shop-bought cinnamon swirl dough for ease. I'm going to add a disclaimer here: because you are cooking in the microwave, you won't get a golden topping on this, but it still tastes absolutely incredible. I love to serve it with a drizzle of my microwave Vanilla Custard (see page 144), a proper naughty dessert!

CINNAMON BUN RAMEKINS

SERVES 4

4 Braeburn apples
    (total weight about
    250 g/9 oz), peeled
    and cut into 1 cm
    (½ inch) cubes
30 g (1 oz) unsalted
    butter, melted
15 g (½ oz) caster sugar
finely grated zest of
    ½ orange
1 × 270 g (9¾ oz) packet
    of cinnamon swirl dough
    (I use Jus-Rol)
icing sugar, to dust
custard, to serve
    (for homemade,
    see page 144)

1. Pop the apples, melted butter, sugar and orange zest into a microwave-safe bowl, cover and cook on full power for 3 minutes, shaking halfway through.

——

2. Remove, stir well, then leave to stand for 2 minutes.

——

3. Divide the cooked apple between 4 ramekins, each about 10 cm (4 inches) in diameter and 5 cm (2 inches) deep.

——

4. Remove the dough from the packet, then cut it into 4 equal-sized rounds. Flatten each piece slightly, then place one into each ramekin, on top of the apple.

——

5. Microwave each ramekin, one at a time, for 3 minutes. Dust with a little icing sugar and serve with custard.

——

18 MINS

 2 MINS

 VEGETARIAN

As a kid, it was a real treat in our house when we had chocolate mousse. More often than not, it was from a packet of 'instant' Angel Delight... If you grew up in the 1980s, like I did, you will know it. My brother and I used to think we were proper little chefs, knocking it up, and it was lush. What I didn't know at the time was how easy it is to make a cheat's chocolate mousse, using just my microwave and a bit of elbow grease to whip up some cream.

CHOCOLATE & HONEYCOMB MOUSSE

SERVES 4
___

100 g (3½ oz) dark chocolate, 70 per cent cocoa solids, broken into pieces
30 g (1 oz) unsalted butter
pinch of salt
300 ml (½ pint) double cream
1 chocolate-coated honeycomb bar, crushed (I use Crunchie)

1. Pop the chocolate into a microwave-safe bowl with the butter and salt. Cook in 20-second bursts until the chocolate has fully melted. Leave to cool for 10 minutes.
___

2. Whip the double cream until it forms soft peaks, but be careful not to over-whip. Reserve one-quarter of the cream for topping the mousse, then gently fold the cooled chocolate through the remaining cream until fully combined.
___

3. Spoon the chocolate mousse into 4 small serving glasses, top with the reserved cream, then cover and chill, if you like.
___

4. Scatter over the crushed honeycomb to serve.
___

Tip
___
Let the mousse come up to room temperature before eating, as this gives it a much better texture.

 3 HOURS 10 MINS

 4½ MINS

 VEGETARIAN

This quick and easy recipe takes inspiration from one of my favourite chocolate bars. As you may know, a Bounty bar comes in two varieties: milk chocolate and dark chocolate. Each to their own, but, for me, dark chocolate wins every time. In this microwave fudge, the combination of a sweet coconut filling with a crisp, bitter outer chocolate shell really is a taste of paradise.

DOUBLE CHOCOLATE COCONUT FUDGE

MAKES 25 PIECES

397 g (14 oz) can of condensed milk
300 g (10½ oz) white chocolate, broken into pieces
80 g (2¾ oz) desiccated coconut
100 g (3½ oz) dark chocolate, 70 per cent cocoa solids, broken into pieces
50 g (1¾ oz) unsalted butter, cubed

1. Line a 20 cm (8 inch) square baking tin with baking parchment.

2. Pour the condensed milk into a microwave-safe bowl, add the white chocolate pieces, then microwave for 3 minutes on full power, stirring halfway through. Stir until the chocolate has completely melted.

3. Scatter in most of the coconut, reserving some for the top, then stir again. Decant the white chocolate mixture into the prepared tin.

4. Pop the dark chocolate and butter into another microwave-safe bowl, then heat on full power for 90 seconds until melted. Stir and check it's all smoothly melted.

5. Drizzle the dark chocolate over the white chocolate, using a palette knife to spread it into an even layer. Sprinkle over the reserved coconut, then leave to cool for 3 hours until set.

6. Cut into 25 equal square pieces to serve.

8 MINS

 40 MINS

 VEGETARIAN

You might well read this recipe and think there must be a typo in the cooking times. There isn't, as it does in fact take quite a while to cook rice pudding in the microwave... but it's still a sight easier and more energy-efficient than doing it the traditional way either on the hob or in the oven. And this classic pudding, full of tropical flavours, is so worth the wait.

MANGO & COCONUT RICE PUDDING

SERVES 4

160 g (5¾ oz) pudding rice
400 g (14 oz) can of full-fat
   coconut milk
40 g (1½ oz) sugar
1 teaspoon vanilla extract
500 ml (18 fl oz) whole milk
1 mango, peeled, stone
   removed, cut into 1 cm
   (½ inch) cubes
60 g (2¼ oz) pistachios,
   crushed
2 tablespoons honey

1. Put the rice, coconut milk, sugar and vanilla extract into a large microwave-safe bowl, cover and cook on full power for 10 minutes.

2. Stir, cover again, then cook for a further 10 minutes.

3. Remove from the microwave and add the milk, stir well, then cover again and cook for a further 20 minutes, stirring halfway through.

4. Portion into bowls, then top with the mango, pistachios and a drizzle of honey to serve.

3 MINS

 2½ MINS

 VEGETARIAN

For those moments when you need something sweet to eat but don't have long to knock it up, I give you my microwave Oreo mug cake. From start to finish, this can be prepared, cooked and ready to eat in about five minutes. The chocolate chips aren't completely necessary, but I just love that combination of hot sponge and melted chocolate, along with the texture you get from the cookies.

OREO MUG CAKE

SERVES 1

———

3 chocolate sandwich
   cookies, such as
   Oreos, crushed
35 g (1¼ oz) self-raising flour
20 g (¾ oz) caster sugar
1 teaspoon cocoa powder
½ teaspoon baking powder
100 ml (3½ fl oz) whole milk
5 g (⅛ oz) chocolate chips
   (optional, see recipe
   introduction)

1. Mix all the dry ingredients together in a microwave-safe mug until fully combined, then add the milk and stir again.

———

2. Cook on full power for 2 minutes.

———

3. Scatter over the chocolate chips, if using, then cook for a further 30 seconds. Leave to stand for 1 minute, then enjoy.

———

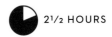 2½ HOURS

 20 MINS

 VEGETARIAN

As a kid, Tuesday evenings were spent at breakdance lessons... yes, I was a 1980s brat and that dance was all the rage. After the lessons, me and my brother Wes would head to a café and order a millionaire's shortbread. It's funny the things that stay with you over the years: for me, more often than not, great memories have a connection with good food. Right, I'm off to get a roll of lino and my boombox; let's see if I've still got those dance moves in me.

SALTED CARAMEL MILLIONAIRE'S SHORTBREAD

SERVES 8

For the base
80 g (2¾ oz) unsalted butter
40 g (1½ oz) caster sugar
150g (5½ oz) plain flour

For the caramel
397 g (14 oz) can of
    condensed milk
80 g (2¾ oz) unsalted
    butter, cubed
80 g (2¾ oz) caster sugar
1 teaspoon sea salt flakes,
    or to taste

For the topping
100 g (3½ oz) dark
    chocolate, 70 per cent
    cocoa solids, broken
    into pieces
40 g (1½ oz) unsalted butter
sea salt flakes (optional)

1. Line a microwave-safe baking dish measuring about 20 × 15 cm (8 × 6 inches) with baking parchment.

2. For the base, pop the butter into a microwave-safe bowl, then heat on full power for 1 minute until melted. Stir through the sugar and flour until combined, then tip into the prepared dish. Use a spoon to flatten the base into an even layer, then cook on full power for 4 minutes. Set aside.

---

3. For the caramel, use the same bowl in which you made the base. Pour in the condensed milk, butter and sugar. Microwave on full power for 8 minutes, stirring after every minute, then cook in 30-second bursts, again stirring in between, for another 2–3 minutes. It should be thicker and a darker colour than when you started. Add the salt to taste, then pour this over the shortbread base. Leave to cool for 2 hours until set.

---

4. Pop the chocolate and butter for the topping into a microwave-safe bowl, then microwave for 1 minute. Stir well, then cook in 20-second bursts until the chocolate has melted. Pour the chocolate over the caramel, then smooth out into an even layer. If you want, sprinkle with a small amount of sea salt flakes.

---

5. Leave to cool fully before cutting into 8 equal-sized pieces.

18 MINS

 6 MINS

 VEGETARIAN

The combination of chocolate and hazelnut is a beautiful thing. Add on top of that a segment of my favourite chocolate bar and I'm in heaven. These five-ingredient cookies can be whipped up in next to no time and cooked in less than a minute. Trust me: you are going to want to try these.

CHOCOLATE HAZELNUT SWEETSHOP COOKIES

MAKES 8

---

80 g (2¾ oz) chocolate
and hazelnut spread,
such as Nutella
70 g (2½ oz) self-raising flour
2 tablespoons milk
pinch of salt
43 g (1½ oz) Kinder Bueno
bar, broken into segments

1. Mix together the chocolate and hazelnut spread, flour, milk and salt in a bowl, then divide into 8 equal portions. Shape each into a ball about 4 cm (1½ inches) in diameter. Use your fingertip to make an impression in the top of each dough ball, then place on a segment of Bueno.

---

2. For best results I cook these one at a time, as they spread out while cooking. Pop a dough ball on a microwave-safe plate lined with a sheet of baking parchment, then cook on full power for 45 seconds.

---

3. Leave to cool for a couple of minutes, then place on a cooling rack for a further 10 minutes.

Tip

As soon as the cookies come out of the microwave, pop them on to a flat surface, then gently swirl them under a large glass while they are still soft, to shape them back to rounds. It doesn't matter if you don't do this though, as they will still taste great.

10 MINS

 4 MINS

 VEGETARIAN

An old-school dessert brought bang up to date with the help of my microwave, which knocks this sponge up in mere minutes. It is such a cool way to bake, and I couldn't believe how easy it was to create this. As we know, treacle sponge needs custard, so you will find my microwave Vanilla Custard recipe on page 144.

GINGER & TREACLE SPONGES

SERVES 4

---

100 g (3½ oz) unsalted butter, softened, plus more for the ramekins
100 g (3½ oz) golden syrup
100 g (3½ oz) caster sugar
100 g (3½ oz) self-raising flour
2 eggs, lightly beaten
1 teaspoon ground ginger
Vanilla Custard (see page 144), to serve

1. Butter the inside of 4 microwave-safe ramekins, each measuring about 10 cm (4 inches) in diameter and 5 cm (2 inches) deep. Weigh 25 g (1 oz) of golden syrup into the base of each.

---

2. Whisk together the butter, sugar, flour, eggs and ground ginger until light and fluffy.

---

3. Spoon the batter equally into the ramekins, cover each with clingfilm, then make a few small holes in each. Cook 2 puddings at a time on full power for 2 minutes.

---

4. Let them stand for 1 minute, then use a knife to loosen the edges before turning the sponges out into bowls and serving with warm vanilla custard.

Tip

Keep the microwaveable plastic ramekins from shop-bought puddings as these are perfect for cooking these little desserts.

INDEX

UK–US GLOSSARY

Aubergines – eggplants
Bacon rashers – bacon slices
Baking parchment – parchment paper
Bacon rashers – bacon slices
Banging – amazing/brilliant/fantastic
Bicarbonate of soda – baking soda
Biscoff spread – speculoos cookie butter
Biscuits – cookies
Black treacle – blackstrap molasses
Caster sugar – superfine sugar
Chestnut mushrooms – cremini mushrooms
Chips – fries
Cider vinegar – apple cider vinegar
Clingfilm – plastic wrap
Coriander leaves – cilantro leaves
   (NB coriander seeds are called
   that in the UK and the US)
Cornflour – corn starch
Courgette – zucchini
Crisps – chips
Desiccated coconut – unsweetened
   shredded coconut
Double cream – heavy cream
Faff – fuss
Golden caster sugar – unrefined
   superfine sugar
Grated – shredded
Green pepper/red pepper –
   green/red bell pepper

Icing sugar – confectioner's sugar
King prawns – jumbo shrimp
Kitchen paper – paper towel
Lush – delicious
Maris Piper potatoes – all-rounder potatoes
Mature cheese – sharp cheese
Mexicana cheese – cheese with added
   bell peppers, garlic salt and chilli,
   Pepper Jack may be substituted
minced meat – ground meat
Muffins – English muffins
Nanny – grandmother
Peckishness – hunger
Plain flour – all-purpose flour
Pork scratchings – pork crunch/pork rinds
Prawns – shrimp
Rolled oats – old-fashioned oats
Scones – biscuits
Self-raising flour – self-rising flour
Spring onions – scallions
Stitched-up – cheated
Stock pot – jellied 'homestyle' stock cube
Streaky bacon – bacon
Swede – rutabaga
Tenderstem broccoli – broccolini
Toastie/toasted sandwich –
   grilled cheese
Tuck in – eat up

THANK YOU

Sometimes in life, I just have to pinch myself to make sure this is all really happening. Those days all those years ago, when I was sat on my digger in my construction job, dreaming about what I was going to make for dinner that evening, seem a lifetime away. I truly can't believe some of the opportunities that have been given to me over the years since I first got into the world of food back in 2006 after MasterChef.

Becoming a cookbook author, for me, was an absolute pipe dream and I still cannot believe I've written six cookbooks. When I first started out, the thought of having a single book with my name and cheesy grin on the front cover was something I truly believed was out of my reach, so I feel so lucky. Of course, these opportunities wouldn't have arrived without the love, help and support of all the people around me who have made this book possible. I want to thank you all but need also to mention a special few.

My amazing wife, Liz, your support for me in everything I do means the world to me. You're always there for me to lend an ear and bounce ideas off. I must bore you to tears, but you never complain. Where would I be without my chief taster? I could tell you that I'd be absolutely nowhere. I love you more than you'll ever know. At the time of writing this we are about to embark on a new and exciting part of our journey together. Baby Edwards is due in December 2023 to make our family complete along with Indie and our Darling Boys Juke and Geronimo. I can't wait for the sleepless nights, ha ha!

My little superstar, Indie. I cannot even begin to tell you how proud you make all of us. You are the perfect role model to your beautiful little sister, Vivvy, who is growing up just like you – although she does have better banter. Keep following your dreams and working hard. I couldn't wish for a better daughter and you will always be my biggest inspiration.

I have a huge and amazing family. Not only do I have amazing parents in Dad, Lynn, Mum and Paul, but also now Vicky and Glenn too. Not forgetting my little brother Wes and sisters Steph, Amber, Georgia and Lauryn. Your support and encouragement mean I can keep pursuing my dream. And my memories of growing up in a foodie family have truly inspired me to push to get to where I am today.

To Borra, Jan, Louise, Megan, Viera and the rest of the team at DML Talent, I'll always be grateful to you for the continuing opportunities that mean I can chase my dream of working in the world of food.

To everyone at Octopus Publishing Group, thank you so much for the continued support and opportunities to write and publish my recipes in your books. Getting my food out there for people to cook at home has always been my biggest passion and driving force and you've given me this amazing opportunity on four occasions. A huge thank you to Leanne, Natalie, Jaz, Lucy and the rest of the team.

Emma and Alex at Smith & Gilmour, it was amazing to have the opportunity to work with you again. Thank you for being patient and listening to me in regards to how I wanted the book to turn out. You are legends and the book looks incredible.

To Tom, Agathe, Troy, Arnaud and Jess for bringing my food to life. This is not an easy task with such a niche subject, but the images far surpassed anything I thought possible. I massively appreciate all of the long hours and the hard work you put into this book. It's nothing short of spectacular.

Finally, thank you to everyone who has supported me through my cooking journey over the last few years. Social media has become a huge part of my work life and to all those supporters who have taken the time to follow me, engage with my content, message me, share pics of your cooking with me and offer me words of encouragement, I'm nothing without you.

ABOUT THE AUTHOR

Dean Edwards made his first TV appearance on BBC's *MasterChef Goes Large* in 2006, an experience that inspired him to pursue a career in food. Since then, he has been a regular on such UK TV shows as ITV's *Lorraine* and *This Morning*, and has amassed a strong community of more than 800K across his social media platforms, where he posts fuss-free recipes for everyday eating. Dean's ethos is that food should be achievable, simple and, above all, taste fantastic, with ingredients that are inexpensive and accessible.

@deanedwardschef

hamlyn

First published in Great Britain in 2023 by Hamlyn,
an imprint of Octopus Publishing Group Ltd
Carmelite House
50 Victoria Embankment
London EC4Y 0DZ
www.octopusbooks.co.uk

An Hachette UK Company
www.hachette.co.uk

Distributed in the US by Hachette Book Group, 1290 Avenue
of the Americas, 4th and 5th Floors, New York, NY 10104

Distributed in Canada by Canadian Manda Group,
664 Annette St, Toronto, Ontario, Canada M6S 2C8

ISBN 978-0-600-63800-1

A CIP catalogue record for this book is available from the British Library.

Printed and bound in China

10 9 8 7 6 5 4 3 2 1

Editorial Director: Natalie Bradley
Senior Editor: Leanne Bryan
Copy Editor: Lucy Bannell
Art Director: Jaz Bahra
Design and Art Direction: Smith & Gilmour
Photographer: Tom Regester
Food Stylist: Troy Willis
Prop Stylist: Agathe Gits
Production Managers: Lucy Carter & Nic Jones